HOPE
for the Hurting

HOPE
for the Hurting

TONY EVANS

PUBLISHING
NASHVILLE, TENNESSEE

978-1-0877-3699-0

Published by B&H Publishing Group
Nashville, Tennessee

Dewey Decimal Classification: 155.9
Subject Heading: PAIN / SUFFERING / JOY AND
SORROW

Unless otherwise noted, all Scripture quotations are
taken from New American Standard Bible (NASB),
copyright © 1960, 1962, 1963, 1968, 1971, 1972,
1973, 1975, 1977, 1995 by The Lockman Foundation.

Also used: English Standard Version (ESV), ESV® Text
Edition: 2016. Copyright © 2001 by Crossway Bibles, a
publishing ministry of Good News Publishers.
Also used: King James Version (KJV), public domain.

Cover design by B&H Publishing Group.
Cover photo by Lauren Guy Photography.

1 2 3 4 5 6 7 • 25 24 23 22 21

ACKNOWLEDGMENTS

I would like to thank Lifeway Christian Resources and B&H Publishing for their long-standing relationship in publishing, events, and film. It is always a joy to get to work on a project with such Spirit-led servants of the King. I especially want to thank Bill Craig for shepherding this relationship over the years. I also want to thank Taylor Combs and Kim Stanford for their work in reviewing and laying out this manuscript. Lastly, I want to thank Heather Hair for her continued dedication to my written library through her collaboration on this manuscript.

CONTENTS

CHAPTER 1

Coming to the Comforter

Life can be painful.
Life hurts.

Life can come with unique challenges, difficulties, bumps, and bruises that leave you lost and drowning in their wake.

It could be a financial disaster. It could come by way of a health issue. Relationships sometimes turn sour. Careers can feel more like doing time than living your life. You might lose a loved one, or two, or three, or more due to sickness or accidents.

Life does hurt. And Jesus knew it would. He said, "In the world you will have tribulation" (John 16:33 ESV). He didn't say "you might" have troubles and difficulties. Jesus said you, and I, *will* have pain, hurt, and struggles.

Sin has made its mark on society in such a dominant way that its repercussions and reverberations are felt everywhere. Some are experienced because they have been caused by us. Others because someone else has committed sins against us. Other pain we experience may simply be due to atmospheric sin that leaves an impact on all those within it. No matter the exact cause, all of sin's effects in this world bring pain.

Like Christmas presents under a tree, life's pain also comes in a variety of shapes and sizes. But unlike those gifts, you don't really want to open them. And you never know what is inside until you do. What's more, one box can often create a domino effect to more of life's pain—ushering in a Pandora's box of problems to face.

I understand firsthand what this type of compounded pain feels like. I know what it is to face one tragedy after another until you begin to dread the next day, simply because you don't know the bad news it may bring.

In a span of less than two years, I lost my brother, my only sister, my sister's husband, two of my nieces, my father, and my wife—all to health issues of one kind or another. At the same time, both of my daughters received cancer diagnoses and had growing health concerns—which were thankfully treated, and they have since recovered from them.

As you can see, I don't speak from a theological position of platitudes on pain. I am writing to you from my heart.

When I talk to you about pain, I'm not telling you solely what is on my mind or what I have studied on the subject. I am telling you what works and what doesn't, addressing it from my experiences. To face life's difficulties with dignity and come out on the other side with grace is one of our greatest challenges we are given on earth.

As a counselor who has counseled thousands of people in pain, I know that some of us face it well. I also know that others succumb to its crushing weight, which only leads to more pain through the compounding consequences of additional poor personal choices.

In this book, I want to give you some spiritual principles to help you face pain and hurt well. There is love and happiness on the other side of it all, if you will learn how to walk through the hurt with both peace and joy.

> To face life's difficulties with dignity and come out on the other side with grace is one of our greatest challenges we are given on earth.

One man showed us how to do this. His name is Paul. He gave us more than spiritual serendipities celebrating God in the good times. He gave us a strategy for surviving and, even more, for thriving in the midst of life's pain. He didn't just give us a hope for tomorrow but also a delight for today. He showed us the importance of not checking out through distractions or numbing ourselves by self-medicating, but rather how to maximize the moments of life's pain for the purposes God has in mind.

The promise of God's Word has never been a guarantee *from* pain and trouble. It has always been a promise to be experienced *in* the hurt itself. God does manifest His victory on our behalf oftentimes by removing the challenge or bringing us through it, but not until He has developed us in it. God will allow us to remain in pain until we are ready to be delivered from it in order that we might learn, grow, and strengthen our spiritual level of maturity.

The great danger in this spiritual adventure called life is that while you and I are passing through the wilderness, we may want to go back to Egypt, like the Israelites who sought to return to slavery rather than face the hardships at hand. Or another danger comes in the desire to loiter in the wilderness and become unproductive. That is often a result of feeling stuck or not knowing where you are going. You may wind up doing nothing in living out your destiny because you are so discouraged by what you are facing and have no energy left to commit to your calling.

Both of these responses to the wilderness of life reflect what most people do. They either long to return to the known trials of the past, or they become ineffective and stagnant in all things spiritual. But God has a greater plan for the pain in your life. He has a purpose in mind.

As a pastor, I wish I could in good faith and in good conscience tell you that if you come to Jesus, it won't rain. You won't have pain. Nothing will hurt and life will be a cakewalk. I wish I could tell you that if you have faith in God and choose to obey Him, serve Him, and love Him, you will have no troubles. I wish I could promise you a life free from difficulty or financial trials. I wish I could say we live in a world of no abuse, no marital discord, no lingering in extended time waiting for a mate who never seems to show up. I wish I could assure you that your life will be free from crises, health issues, and disappointments.

> God has a greater plan for the pain in your life.

It would make my job a lot easier as a pastor if I could tell you those things. But it would also make me a liar. Because those things are simply not true. They have never been true, and they never will be true.

My role as a spiritual leader in a world rife with pain is to tell the truth, the whole truth, and nothing but the truth. The reason I must do this is because only the Truth will set you free (John 8:32).

The apostle Paul took his commitment to telling the truth seriously too. That's why we read in his own words a pretty stark summation of his life, showing how God has cared for him amidst a mass of suffering, as found in 2 Corinthians 1. Some highlights include:

"[God] comforts us in all our affliction" (v. 4).

"The sufferings of Christ are ours in abundance" (v. 5).

"In the patient enduring of the same sufferings which we also suffer" (v. 6).

"You are sharers of our sufferings" (v. 7).

"We were burdened excessively, beyond our strength, so that we despaired even of life" (v. 8).

"We had the sentence of death within ourselves" (v. 9).

"[God] delivered us from so great a peril of death" (v. 10).

Reading what he's written, you might get the impression that Paul is in a painful situation. Not only that, he's with others whom he cares about who are in painful situations as well.

Have you ever experienced a time when witnessing the pain a loved one felt was deeper than your own pain? When we see our loved ones in pain and we are helpless to remove that pain or relieve them of the burden they are experiencing, it can hurt our hearts just as deeply, if not more so, than painful experiences we have ourselves.

Paul was in pain. His heart hurt. His friends' hearts hurt too. So much so, that he even spoke of wanting to die.

In contemporary language, that would be classified as severe depression. There's no way to sugarcoat someone writing that they "despaired even of life." And yet, what I find interesting in all of this is that Paul is also probably the most mature Christian who has ever lived. He stands head and shoulders above most others when it comes to boldly declaring the faith, representing Jesus, and suffering for His cause. His own descriptions of everything he went through and endured as a follower of Christ are daunting. It's difficult to conceive that one man can go through so much, but Paul did.

The reason I'm pointing this fact out as we start our journey together is because I want to remind all of us whose hearts may hurt that we are not talking about a bad man in pain when we reference Paul and learn from him. We are looking at a good man hurting. A godly man hurting. Even a man hurting as a result of the things he was doing to advance God's kingdom in the world!

See, a lot of believers think that if they follow Jesus, serve Him, and love Him, they are not supposed to hurt. They point fingers at God when something goes wrong. But God never promised any of us a rose garden life or a stroll-through-the-park existence. Nor is every trial we face a personal indictment on our faith.

This world comes with trouble. It just does. The sooner we can accept that reality and stop ourselves from trying to spiritualize every painful situation, loss, or difficulty we encounter, we will be better positioned to weather it well.

People get sick on this planet. People die. People get abused. Go hungry. Lose relationships. Accidents happen. Careers go south. Loneliness lingers. As I referenced earlier, Jesus reminded us that this world comes with troubles and tribulations (John 16:33). But the difference for kingdom followers comes in knowing that because Jesus is in us, we can overcome the onslaught of hurtful scenarios we face.

Other biblical characters understood and wrote about hurtful seasons as well. Probably the most well-known is Job. During his darkest days, he said that he did not sense God's presence. Even though he was known as a righteous man, he felt alone, lost, and in pain. In Job 23 we read: "Behold, I go forward but He is not there, and backward, but I cannot perceive Him; when He acts on the left, I cannot behold Him; He turns on the right, I cannot see Him" (vv. 8–9).

Don't be fooled. Life does hurt. There are different levels at different times for different people, but suffering is something we all share. We all cry. No matter how much we love Jesus, we all find ourselves in times of tears and sorrow, even periods of depression. But like Paul, who had even reached what many

> Because Jesus is in us, we can overcome the onslaught of hurtful scenarios we face.

would term a suicidal level of depression, having "despaired of life itself," we can discover how to dignify our difficulties through one key decision: *focusing on God*. It is in God where we will find the comfort we need. Paul reminds us of this time and again in the same chapter, 2 Corinthians 1, where he outlines his pains and struggles. We read:

"God of all comfort" (v. 3).

"Who comforts us in all our affliction" (v. 4).

"We ourselves are comforted by God" (v. 4).

"Our comfort is abundant through Christ" (v. 5).

"If we are comforted, it is for your comfort" (v. 6).

"You are sharers of our comfort" (v. 7).

Comfort.

God comforts those who need it most.

Many of us have comforters on our beds in our homes. These are thicker blankets designed to provide an extra layer of warmth when needed. The comforter you may have on your bed does not, in and of itself, change the weather. Instead, it changes the effect of the weather on you. It is called a comforter because, if you wrap yourself in it, the cool air that surrounds you no longer has the final say-so on how you feel. Not because the cool air has changed or gotten warmer. If it's chilly in your room, then it's still chilly. But you are now warm because of the warmth of the comforter around or over you.

The Greek word for "comforter" used in the verses we just looked at is the word *paraclete*. It is the same root term used about the Holy Spirit when Jesus said God will send us someone to "help" us in John 14:16: "I will ask the Father, and He will give you another Helper, that He may be with you forever."

Thus, in every affliction, trouble, hurt, pain, distress, or difficulty of life that you may be facing, there is a comforter on the bed. There is a blanket of blessing if you will choose to grab it.

Now, it's possible to spend so much time in a cold room complaining about the cold, all the while not choosing to pull the comforter up over you. It's not because the comforter isn't there; it's because your focus is on the temperature in the room.

Where you choose to focus will affect what you get to experience. If you can only be happy when there are no problems and issues at hand, then your misplaced focus will never allow you to be truly happy. As 1 Corinthians 10:13 states: "God is faithful, who will not allow you to be tempted beyond what you are able, but with the temptation will provide the way of escape also, so that you will be able to endure it." The operative word we often bypass in that verse is *with*. God will provide the way of escape "with" the temptation you face. It doesn't say God will block all temptations from your life. Nor will He block all the challenging situations you face. But He will give you the ability to have joy *with* those challenges.

As we all know, pain and difficulties can be temptations. They exist as temptations to give up, blame God, complain, gripe, blame others, and more. God never promised us a life without temptation or grief. What He did promise is that in the midst of the affliction and hurt, He will give us comfort.

When my kids were younger, my wife, Lois, and I would sometimes take them to the amusement park. They loved the roller coasters and other rides.

The problem with these rides is that other people loved them too. So we would always have to wait in a long line, usually in the Texas heat, in order to ride for a minute or two. Every so often there might be a sign that let us know how much longer our wait time would be.

Eventually, though, the amusement park management got clever. They began to put digital screens up along the way so that as everyone would wait in line, there would be some form of entertainment along the way. On the screens would be various short shows, songs, or glimpses at other rides. They didn't change the wait time—it was still a challenging part of the journey itself. You were still waiting ninety minutes or more to get on the ride. But what they did change was the nature of the wait. Now there was something for you to focus on that took your mind off the pain of having to stand there for so long.

I don't know how long God is going to keep you in the line you are in. I don't know how long He is going to make you wait for your deliverance to come. I can't guarantee you that your problem is going to be solved tomorrow, next month, or even next year. You can pray toward that end, trust toward that end, and desire toward that end, but you and I both know that neither of us can create that end on our own.

So I'm not going to spend my time and yours in this book making false promises to you that if you trust Jesus, Monday is going to be better. For all I know, Monday may even be worse. But what I will tell you is that while you are waiting for the pain to subside and the hurt to heal, there is a Comforter given to you by God. God has offered you a new focus of His own divinity to take your focus off your own feet standing still for so long. There is something God has provided you while you are in this line called life, and it is designed to equip and enable you to deal with all you are facing right now.

If you will choose to look to God in the midst of your affliction by giving a theological focus to the troubles you face, you will give dignity to your difficulty and provide purpose to your pain. God isn't asking you to like the hurt you are feeling; He is asking you to accept that it has a greater meaning and intention in His hands. God does not give you pain just for pain's sake.

Here's a very simple principle to apply as you walk through the ups and downs of life: the worse the pain gets, the deeper your focus on the Lord ought to be. You can do this when you rest in the overarching reality of the sovereignty of God.

The sovereignty of God means that nothing happens to you unless it passes through God's fingers first. God is in control. Either God has caused what has happened to you, or He has allowed it. If He caused it, He has a reason for it. If He has allowed it, you also need to trust the truth that His allowance has a cause in and of itself, as stated in Romans 8:28, "And we know that God causes all things to work together for good to those who love God, to those who are called according to His purpose." The core of God's purpose is to increase and expedite our conformity to the image of Christ (v. 29). Making us more like Jesus is God's ultimate purpose for every believer. Everything that happens is supernaturally designed with the overarching goal of enhancing our spiritual development.

> The worse the pain gets, the deeper your focus on the Lord ought to be.

Never underestimate the sovereignty of God. If something reached you, it passed through Him first. Therefore, if it passed through Him by Him allowing it to reach you, He let it get to you for a reason. It's never aimless, random, a result of bad luck or chance. None of those words ought to be part of a serious Christian's vocabulary. Those are empty, meaningless terms when a sovereign God controls all things.

Like the three Hebrew boys left in the fiery furnace, God doesn't always deliver you out of difficulty. Sometimes He chooses to join you in it (Dan. 3:25). The fire stayed hot. But the effect of the fire no longer had a damaging impact on the three young men because God had entered the equation.

If God has not taken you out of whatever it is you are facing right now, know that He wants to join you in it. Let Him in. Let Him come near. Ask Him to reveal Himself to you in the middle of what you are going through. He has the power to limit the damaging effects of whatever it is you are facing or dealing with right now.

Knocked Down but
Not Knocked Out

Things may not change entirely when you draw near to God in the middle of painful situations, but the way you experience them will change. We see how this comes about in 2 Corinthians 4:6–11 where Paul explains it more fully. It says:

> For God, who said, "Light shall shine out of darkness," is the One who has shone in our hearts to give the Light of the knowledge of the glory of God in the face of Christ.
>
> But we have this treasure in earthen vessels, so that the surpassing greatness of the power will be of God and not from ourselves; we are afflicted in every way, but not crushed; perplexed, but not despairing; persecuted, but not forsaken; struck down, but not destroyed; always carrying about in the body the dying of Jesus, so that the life of Jesus also may be manifested in our body. For we who live are constantly being delivered over to death for Jesus' sake, so that the life of Jesus also may be manifested in our mortal flesh.

Paul points out to you and me in this passage that even when circumstances may knock us down, they shouldn't knock us out. When you are going through the affliction, that is the time to run to God like never before. God must be free to work in you before He can work for you.

Too often our prayers go something like this: "God, please work for me by changing my situation." All the while, God smiles and responds like a caring parent: "I hear you and I understand your request. But I can't work for you until you let me work in you. I'm trying to develop something in you so that what I am doing will show up and produce the desired result."

Any woman who has given birth understands there can be a great purpose to pain. The hurt can be extreme. What's more, it can last for hours. But in the pain, hurt, and difficulties of labor, there is often someone to give comfort. It might be some cool water or a kind word. It could be a piece of ice or a gentle massage. Someone is there who loves you and will offer comfort to you in order to help you get through the pain of giving birth.

In our spiritual lives we also give birth. We give birth to maturity, new dreams, victory over sin, vision, love, and Christlike purpose through the pain we experience. As a kingdom follower you have to understand that something unique occurs through the trials of life that could never occur in the times of great blessing. Growth happens in the midst of grit and grind.

What you need to do in the middle of it all is remember that God knows right where you are and sees what you are going through. He wants to birth something in you and through you that will reveal Christ at an even greater level than before. Yet without a focus on Jesus Christ, the pain is only painful, not purposeful.

> Growth happens in the midst of grit and grind.

Seek His comfort, not just the exit. His comfort is there for you right now.

But how can you get even more comfort than you have experienced up to this point? Paul tells us in one of the passages we looked at earlier. Let's examine it more closely because it is critical. He writes: "[God] comforts us in all our affliction so that we will be able to comfort those who are in any affliction with the comfort with which we ourselves are comforted by

God" (2 Cor. 1:4). The bottom-line principle is this: God comforts you so that you can become a comforter of someone else.

In the midst of your pain, you need to look for someone else to comfort as well. God reveals to us in this passage that He comforts us so that we might comfort others. So, while you are needing comfort yourself, you also need to look at how your greater understanding of pain, hurt, and difficulties has increased your compassion for others, especially those who are suffering in a similar situation to your own.

Now, I understand firsthand that one of the hardest things to do when you are hurting is to think of someone else. This is because you are dealing with your own pain.

One of our church members told me about a funeral that was held for her mother not too long ago. An interesting thing stood out to her during the planning and the funeral itself. She said that every time they met with her mother's pastor at the church she had attended and who would be conducting the funeral, he would ask her and her family members to pray for him. He would even go on to give some specific things to pray about. This happened every time, even if they just spoke in passing. This pastor would always end the conversation by asking them to pray for him.

At first, she said she just brushed this off as a formality. Then she started to wonder if anyone could truly be that selfish. But later, when it happened enough times, she started to ponder why he would be asking this of them so regularly, knowing they were overwhelmed with personal grief and trauma.

It dawned on her that he was trying to remind them to focus on someone else. Just like 2 Corinthians 1:4 says, we are given comfort in order to comfort others. This pastor had given many words of comfort and many prayers of comfort throughout the planning of the funeral and the actual funeral itself. He hadn't been dismissive of their pain at all. His prayer request was simply a gentle reminder to let comfort flow through them rather than to bottle it up and become stagnant and self-absorbed.

One of the fastest paths to healing from your hurt is to help someone else even while you are still hurting. This seasoned and wise pastor understood this spiritual truth and was seeking to help her and her family heal. Thinking about someone else is one of the hardest things to do when you are hurting, but it is one of the best things to do when you are hurting. Why? Because the comfort you give is the comfort you will receive. That's why it is always "more blessed to give than to receive" (Acts 20:35).

Similar to food, emotions must also pass through you for you to be healthy. If you choose to live as a cul-de-sac Christian, you'll wind up a very constipated Christian! If all you think about is what comes *to* you but not about what can flow *through* you, you will make yourself sick.

God has designed each of us to provide comfort to others as we also look to be comforted ourselves. In fact, He will often allow our pain in order that we might develop a deeper level of compassion and empathy for those who are also experiencing pain themselves.

> The comfort you give is the comfort you will receive.

As we walk through this topic together in these brief pages, you're going to learn how God has a special lane for comforters. It's similar to the HOV lane on a crowded highway. If you choose to travel alone, you'll be stuck in the misery of the mess of bumper-to-bumper cars. But if you pair up with someone else who also needs to get where you are going—to a place of healing and hope—you will enter the HOV lane and travel more quickly and smoothly.

I have some boxes in my garage where some people sent me gifts this past Christmas. The boxes had cushioning material in them so the contents inside wouldn't get all shaken up and broken. Thus, as the box was tossed around and thrown around, being transported from station to station on train or truck, the gifts inside remained protected. Now, the foam didn't stop the boxes or the gifts inside from being bounced around. It just stopped them from being jacked up, having been bounced around. It prevented them from getting busted or broken.

Now, if you are anything like me and like to save your money rather than waste it, you'll have those boxes with that foam stacked somewhere in the garage. The reason is because when it comes time for me to mail something, I can reuse both the box and the foam. I can take the comforter around the gift that was sent to me, and I can use it to protect what I send to someone else. In this way, whatever I send will also be able to handle the jerking and shifting that come its way.

This is what Paul is trying to tell us. He's trying to show us that God comforts us during periods of difficulties and disasters so that we can then use that same comfort to instill hope and healing in others. A perfect example of this is given to us in 2 Corinthians 7:5–7 where Paul pens: "For even when we came into Macedonia our flesh had no rest, but we were afflicted on every side: conflicts without, fears within. But God, who comforts the depressed, comforted us by the coming of Titus; and not only by his coming, but also by the comfort with which he was comforted in you, as he reported to us your longing, your mourning, your zeal for me; so that I rejoiced even more."

> The primary way God comforts people is through people.

The primary way God comforts people is through people. God calls upon those who can feel, see, and understand to supply His comfort to others. He uses those who can identify with the pain others are experiencing so that the comfort they give them is authentic and real.

Let me put it in plain, everyday language for you: you cannot expect to experience God like you want to without also ministering to others.

If you attend Worship Selfish at church rather than Worship Service, your experience of God will be self-limiting.

If your Christian faith is only about how you can be blessed or comforted, your experience of God will be constricted.

If you only care about getting out of your painful circumstance as fast as possible and not helping others in the midst of their painful circumstances, your experience of God will be short-circuited.

One of the great truths of Scripture is that God must first remove our self-reliance, self-focus, and self-sufficiency before He can lift us to the position of our destiny. We often call this *brokenness*, where we no longer depend upon ourselves because we can no longer depend upon ourselves. In other words, you are broken when your options have run out, there's nothing left to do, you don't know where to go, and you don't have a contact who can help you. Even your money can't buy your way out. Your energy is spent, and you are just flat-out done.

This may sound like a bad place to be. But the moment you know you are done is the moment when you have reached the perfect position to experience your life's purpose. Because it is then, and only then, that God is able to get the glory and credit He is due. God will sometimes allow us to reach the point of emotional and experiential death in our lives so that we will no longer trust ourselves, but rather we will trust in the One who is able to raise the dead.

That's why personal peace and hope always start with the praise and honor of God. In the midst of whatever you are facing right now—whatever it is that drew you to this book or caused you to pick it up and read it—I want you to choose to praise God.

Choose to worship God.

Choose to trust God.

Choose to believe that God is able to take your mess and make a miracle.

He is able to take your lemons and turn them into sweet lemonade. God is able to take your bitter and make it better. He can turn your dreary yesterdays into brighter tomorrows. *But you have to let Him.* You have to allow Him into the mire and muck of your pain, hurt, and sorrow so that He can show you the way out. He's not going to rescue you out of every painful scenario. But He has shown you how, by your own choices and ministry to others according to His will, you can be lifted up and discover the hope and comfort for which you long.

CHAPTER 2

Discovering the Treasure Within

I'm sure many of us have expensive things in cheap containers in our homes. You might have rings that cost you a lot to purchase being stored in something that didn't cost that much at all. That inexpensive container holds a vast treasure of significant value.

Similarly, inside each of us is a treasure of unlimited value. Paul writes about this in 2 Corinthians 4:7, "But we have this treasure in earthen vessels, so that the surpassing greatness of the power will be of God and not from ourselves."

Paul speaks of a treasure we have within our earthen vessels. It's a treasure inside of our body. In biblical days, the term *earthen vessel* would refer to a clay pot or jar. Inside of that pot would often be placed something extremely valuable. By using this as an example, Paul was pointing out that what is inside of our bodies—bodies that can break down and be beaten down, worn out, and seem unimpressive—is something incredibly valuable.

Far too often we get caught up on the container—our external lives—while missing the value and eternal nature of who we truly are in Christ. This is why Paul took the time to remind us of what matters most. He wants us to make the most of our difficulties and hurts in life so that we benefit from them rather than simply endure them.

Paul tells us more clearly what this treasure is in the verse right before his reference to the earthen vessels. We read in 2 Corinthians 4:6 what he says: "For God, who said, 'Light shall shine out of darkness,' is the One who has shone in our hearts to give the Light of the knowledge of the glory of God in the face of Christ." Located inside of you and me is the knowledge of God.

Now, knowledge does not only refer to information. It refers to an experience of God. It is the very presence of God Himself inside each of us. This hidden treasure of immense value exists in all who trust in Jesus Christ for the forgiveness of sins and for eternal life.

If you could go up to God and talk to Him face-to-face, wouldn't that be considered a treasure? That would be something of inestimable value. But we *do* have this ability. Each of us does. Within our bodies—our earthen vessels—is a treasure consisting of the love and light of God. This treasure just needs to be unwrapped to be accessed more fully. Hardships, difficulties, and brokenness often help us in unwrapping the treasure found within because they take our eyes off ourselves and turn our focus toward Jesus.

To put it another way, the closer you get to Christ, the more of God you get to experience. Colossians 2:2–3, 9–10 puts it like this: "that their hearts may be encouraged, having been knit together in love, and attaining to all the wealth that comes from the full assurance of understanding, resulting in a true knowledge of God's mystery, that is, Christ Himself, in whom are hidden all the treasures of wisdom and knowledge. . . . For in Him all the fullness of Deity dwells in bodily form, and in Him you have been made complete, and He is the head over all rule and authority."

In other words, Christ is God with skin on. Jesus is God's selfie. He came that we may know God more fully and in a more personal way. So, if you want to unwrap the treasure of God in you, just look to Jesus Christ. When you look to Christ and connect with Him, you get all the wisdom and knowledge there is to have because all of that is located in Jesus. As you draw nearer to Jesus during the hurts and pains of this life, you will experience God the way He desires to be experienced by you.

> The closer you get to Christ, the more of God you get to experience.

You've probably seen the majesty of a wild stallion running free. He runs with strength and power. But there is only one way to bring that power into submission to a rider, and that is through a process called "breaking." To break a horse is to work with the horse until they learn that you are not going to let up until they surrender to you. Once a horse is broken, the power and majesty within it now can be guided and directed with ease. It is power under control.

God longs for us to maximize the majesty and power He's given to us and not just let it exist with no direction from Him. Brokenness often ushers in a humility that will enable us as believers to surrender to Him. In this way, His power is made greater in us, and our power and majesty are displayed to a greater degree through the destiny He has in store for us in the treasure He's given to each of us.

This spectacular possession is within us. You need to look within. Keep in mind that far too often we get hung up on the external package of this life. But on our best days, we are nothing more than dignified dirt. We're dressed-up, got-our-hair-done, driving-a-nice-car-while-living-in-a-nice-house dirt. The treasure is *within* us. It is not in the external world or even made up of our bodies. The treasure is inside.

You cannot always measure the value of something by what you see. In fact, you usually can't. Not too long ago, I attended a special conference as the guest speaker where all the attendees were either multimillionaires or billionaires. Now, I had to be told that information because, by looking at everyone in attendance, you wouldn't have known. The attendees looked like everyday normal people to me. That's because when you look at the external, you don't always see what there is behind the persona. The external is rarely an authentic reflection of everything that goes into who that person truly is.

What Paul is trying to tell us through the passages we have read so far is that this experience of the knowledge of God—this treasure that God has placed in every believer—has been so situated within that it cannot be manifested by our own power. It must be the reflection of God's power.

It's not about who you are or who you know. It's not even about what you own or have access to. In fact, nothing will keep this experience of God further from you than you looking to yourself to produce it. Why? Because that's called pride, and God hates pride. The moment you move independently of God, you have moved away from the treasure within.

Yet the reason so many of us move toward ourselves and away from God is because we want to avoid pain. We want to avoid the process of growth. We seek to remove ourselves from situations that cause or allow us to be crushed. But Paul reminds us that access to the life of Christ within us comes through attachment to His sufferings.

Life brings problems. But what we often forget or fail to realize is that these problems often exist in order that the life of Jesus might be made manifest in our mortal bodies. This is why Paul wanted to participate in the fellowship of Jesus' sufferings (Phil. 3:10).

Paul outlines this for us when he follows up 2 Corinthians 4:7, which we read at the start of this chapter, with the next three explanatory verses. He says: "We are afflicted in every way, but not

> The moment you move independently of God, you have moved away from the treasure within.

crushed; perplexed, but not despairing; persecuted, but not forsaken; struck down, but not destroyed; always carrying about in the body the dying of Jesus, so that the life of Jesus also may be manifested in our body" (vv. 8–10).

It is only when we connect the preeminent and valuable treasure within to the process of accessing that treasure (carrying about in the body the dying of Jesus) that we get to experience the life of Jesus made manifest. I realize that it would be much easier for all of us if we could just cut those three verses from truth and reality. In that way we could move right onto celebration.

But life doesn't work that way.

Life has not been designed that way. In fact, just the opposite is true. If there is no dying (identifying with the death of Christ), then there is no living. The way we are to experience the fullness of life is through death. Whether that means the death of wrong desires, sinful passions, misplaced trust, illicit ideas, or even simply the death of the need for security, predictability, and stability—death must take place before true life comes forth.

When you and I are seeking to unwrap the treasure of the experiential knowledge of God by looking at the face of Christ, we must be willing to identify with Christ. God will often allow circumstances in our lives that are painful in order to help us see Jesus more authentically and identify with Him more completely.

Problems can sometimes be designed to kill something within us that needs to be removed. This can be compared to how the heat of an oven is designed to kill the bacteria that could harm us in raw meat. While the meat is hot in the oven, it isn't done until the internal portions have been cooked thoroughly. Some people will stick a knife or a fork in the meat to test it. Others might put a meat thermometer in it to let them know when it's done. This is because if the meat is not done on the inside, it can be dangerous to whoever eats it.

Now, if the meat could talk, it would remind you that it is very hot and uncomfortable in the oven. It might remind you that 450 degrees doesn't feel all that good. But none of that talk and complaining would matter to you because, as the person cooking the meat, it's your job to make sure it is safe for those who consume it. Your purposes overrule those of the meat itself.

Similarly, God's purposes for our lives rank higher than our own. He has a reason for the fiery trials and difficulties we face. It is through the heat of hurt and suffering that we are often refined when the bacteria of sin are put to death.

It is important that these sins are put to death because they may be getting in the way of you coming into a full experiential knowledge of God through Christ. It could be pride or an unhealthy need for control. It could be pleasure or an obsession with ease. It could be something as simple, yet still as sinful, as selfishness. Whatever is keeping you from experiencing God must go. It must die. It must be removed so that you stand before Him stripped, honest, and authentic.

> Whatever is keeping you from experiencing God must go.

Like old paint or varnish on a piece of furniture, there are seasons when our souls need to be stripped of that which is covering up the beauty of the treasure within.

If you, like me, enjoy eating roasted peanuts, then you know where the good stuff is actually found. You know that it is not in the shell itself. I have never seen anyone get excited about a nutshell. In fact, the shell is discarded as fast as possible. That's because the person eating the peanuts wants the treasure inside. But for the treasure to be accessed, the shell has to be damaged. It has to be broken. It has to be ripped off and removed.

God has a treasure in you, and He doesn't want you to block its full expression. Because of this, He will sometimes allow things to come into your life that may be painful, inconvenient, and difficult to endure, but He does this so that the "life of [Christ]" (2 Cor. 4:10) may be made increasingly more evident in all you do and say.

Brokenness is often the road to breakthrough. Although we'd like to, we can't skip verses 8 and 9 of 2 Corinthians and jump to verse 10. When God allows the troubles we face, we must face them.

Negative experiences are designed to give us a new level of experience with God. Jesus is never more real to us than in those times when life does not seem to be working out.

You remember the old-fashioned piggy banks we used to have as kids? You would drop your coins into the slit at the top in order to store your change. But when you wanted to redeem your money from inside the pig, you would have to turn it upside down and shake it like there's no tomorrow. I'm sure you can remember how frustrating it was when the money wouldn't come out easily. In fact, some people even broke open their piggy bank by smashing it to get their treasure out.

Similarly, God has placed a treasure in you and me, in earthen vessels. He wants the treasure to be made manifest. He wants it to come out. Sometimes He must flip us over and shake us. Other times He has to turn us around and let things rattle a bit inside. Then there are even those times when we must be broken to release the treasure within.

Here's a life tip: breaking usually takes place when we refuse to cooperate with the shaking. One way we frequently refuse is through keeping ourselves so distracted and numbed from our pain that we fail to face it in order to let it do its work in us.

Do you know what the big idol in American culture is today? The badge of being busy. We use distractions in order to numb ourselves from the pain and emptiness we feel. This is one of the reasons that the rate of depression, anxiety, alcohol abuse, and pornography use skyrocketed during the onset and height of the 2020 pandemic lockdown. When people lost their opportunities to be busy, life's pain had to be faced head-on. That proved to be too much for many of us.

I can identify with this in a lot of ways. As I mentioned earlier, 2019 was the hardest year of my life. I lost my father and my wife, along with other family members who went home to be with the Lord. I limped into 2020 with a heavy heart, full of pain and hurt.

But then when the lockdown came about, I found myself sitting home even more. I couldn't use busyness as a distraction from what I was feeling. In fact, having gotten pneumonia in the early part of the lockdown, I found myself staying home all the time—in the very same home I had shared with my wife for decades— day after day, week after week.

Memories met my every glance. My wife's hats remained stacked in the closets, just as she had left them. Photos were left out in frames, everywhere—on walls and countertops. We decided as a family to not get rid of anything right away, but rather to keep it as it was in her honor and memory. And while that has been good, it has also been very hard. Every glance could produce either glory or a grimace. Glory in the celebration of who she was and what she meant to me. Or a grimace of pain in the reminder of the beautiful and loving partner I no longer have near me.

In the midst of these hurtful days, I had to make a choice. I could fixate on the devastation that I felt or I could choose to turn to Christ for His help to make it through.

It was a daily choice because, as anyone going through suffering and pain knows, you must take it one day at a time.

I did choose to draw near to God. I sought the One who provides comfort when comfort is needed most.

I'll admit, I did have some help in making that choice. My family surrounded me with loving reminders to stay present and engaged. I was rarely, if ever, alone. My family dedicated their time to filling my days with their love. And then, before I knew it, just a few months after losing my wife of nearly fifty years—our entire nation and the world fell into a crisis as well.

In fact, as the year rolled on, we began to face multiple pandemics—health, racial, societal, and political. As a pastor, people were looking to me to lead them through it. They wanted insight on how to process all that was going on, as well as how to respond emotionally from a spiritual perspective. Meanwhile, I needed help myself, struggling through all the losses I was enduring.

These pandemics pulled me from a place of sulking into a place of serving. As I served others in the middle of my own personal pain, I began to witness the slow but steady healing of my own heart as well. This is how God works in us. As we experience the death of that which we value and hold so dear to us in order to grasp that which Christ values and holds so dear to Him— that call to love Him and serve others—we experience His strength in our heart and His hope in our spirit. We experience comfort. We find hope.

What to Do While Waiting on Hope

Not only do we discover hope in our own helping of others, but Paul gives us more insight into how we can obtain it when we need it most. Looking further into the passage we read: "But having the same spirit of faith, according to what is written, 'I BELIEVED, THEREFORE I SPOKE,' we also believe, therefore we also speak" (2 Cor. 4:13). In this verse, Paul tells us what we are to do while we are waiting on our hope to return. He says that while you are going through the difficulties you are facing, check what is written in Scripture on it, and then speak it. Profess the truths of God's Word over your own life. In the words of the psalmist, David, encourage yourself in the Lord (Ps. 42). Let your mouth and your belief say the same thing, and let them both agree with what God says is true.

In other words, speak God's Word to your situation.

When you are going through something you don't want to go through, encourage yourself with truth. Far too often we cancel our faith with what we say. We will say the opposite of what God says in Scripture. Through our complaining, postulating, and worrying, we confirm a lie rather than the truth. Yet God can only set you free with the truth (John 8:30–32). You must speak truth to your spirit during the difficult, dark days. Don't be double-minded. It's Truth that will set you free—not your version of truth.

> Profess the truths of God's Word over your own life.

You also need to be intentional of your surroundings. Choose to hang out with other people who are speaking truth too—and not their versions of truth either. If you decide to phone a friend who is just talking noise—encouraging you to complain, give up, or gossip—you are holding back what God is trying to do. Your own words are canceling out your blessing.

Did you know that you can abort your own abundance? Every time you speak about how bad things are, or how little money you have, or how you just don't know if you can make it, you are affirming the lies of the enemy. God's promises are truth. You may not feel like they are true, but they are true. Let your words reflect His truth, not your emotions. When you do that, your emotions will soon get aligned with truth as well.

Always speak that which is true, biblical, and from God's point of view. You can be as confident as Paul when you do. Paul spoke truth in the middle of his darkest days because he knew that "He who raised the Lord Jesus will raise us also with Jesus and will present us with you. For all things are for your sakes, so that the grace which is spreading to more and more people may cause the giving of thanks to abound to the glory of God" (2 Cor. 4:14–15).

Paul talks of this grace causing others to give thanks, which brings light to the glory of God. Grace has a purpose. Grace is God's provision of all the spiritual blessings in the heavenly places (Eph. 1:3). When we receive His grace, it produces gratitude within us. It causes us to not lose heart. It nudges us to keep going. In fact, Paul tells us exactly this as his words of encouragement conclude this chapter: "Therefore we do not lose heart, but though our outer man is decaying, yet our inner man is being renewed day by day. For momentary, light affliction is producing for us an eternal weight of glory far beyond all comparison, while we look not at the things which are seen, but at the things which are not seen; for the things which are seen are temporal, but the things which are not seen are eternal" (2 Cor. 4:16–18).

In these verses, Paul reminds us that the way our lives are supposed to work is that, even though we are getting older each day, we are to be getting younger on the inside at the same time. Our inward man, where the treasure of knowing God fully is located, should be renewed through every experience we have.

The outward man may decay. And does. You've probably noticed it like I have. I know I have to sit down and rest more than I ever did before, now that I'm in my seventies. But regardless of what our physical body becomes, our inward man—the treasure of our God connection—should stay young. Affliction and pain produce within us an "eternal weight of glory" (v. 17), which is to transmute the hurt into hope . . . if you let it.

I find Paul's choices of words interesting in this last passage. He uses terms like *momentary* and *light* when describing pain. This, coming from a man who acknowledged he was at the point of wanting to give up entirely! But what he is encouraging us to remember is that if the suffering seems long or heavy or burdensome, it is because we are looking at what we can see. We are fixating too fully on the temporal reality we are in right now. And if all you see is what you see, you do not see all there is to be seen.

> If all you see is what you see, you do not see all there is to be seen.

Now, Paul isn't saying we should deny the reality of our hurt or circumstances. But he is saying we should shift our focus. How you view the trials and troubles of life will determine how you feel about them. If you are staring only at the affliction, you are not looking at the "eternal weight of glory" (v. 17) being produced by it. We are to gaze beyond the affliction to the glory. We are to look beyond the hurt to the healing, which Jesus is bringing about through a greater manifestation of His presence within us. We are to see past the temporary into eternity.

If you compare a minute to an hour, it could seem long. If you compare a minute to a day, it could still seem significant. But if you compare it to a decade or even to eternity, it will be but a blip on the screen of your life. Time feels relative.

Do you remember how it was when you were younger, and it felt like it would be forever before you would finally turn eighteen? But then once you reached adulthood, somehow the years just flew by. It's almost as if the second hand started skipping minutes and hours altogether. But you know as well as I do that time didn't change. The clock didn't move any differently. It's just that we began viewing time through another perspective. When you are on the early end of time, it ticks and tocks very slowly. When you are on the later end of time, you can barely seem to keep up.

How you view what you are facing will change how you feel about what you are facing. When you place your pain and your hurt in the grid of God's grace and His glory, you will discover the peace that surpasses understanding.

Let me tell you an easy way to start changing how you view things. You can begin by practicing what you say and how you say it, as Paul urged us earlier on. It all hinges on the word *but*, and where you choose to place it. If you say, "God is good, but life is bad," your focus will be on what is bad. Yet if you say, "Life is bad, but God is good," your focus will be on the goodness of God. You can flip your emotions by flipping the order of what you say. Always end with God, and you'll be able to handle whatever it is you begin with.

It's like the story of a man who was at the filling station and the attendant started to clean his windshield. When he finished cleaning it, the driver asked him to go back and do it again. He told him he had done a poor job, and his windshield was still dirty. The man went back and cleaned it again, but even this time the driver was not satisfied with the result. That was until the attendant pointed out that the man may need to clean his own glasses. After cleaning his own glasses, his own field of vision, he could see that the windshield in front of him had been clean all along.

If you insist on looking at life's hurt and your heart's pain through your own human lenses, you will continue to see a mess. You will not see all there is to be seen. My challenge to you in the midst of our world's messes is to pray for God's perspective. Ask for His viewpoint. Align your sight with His sight so that you can see what He is doing rather than what the world reflects or projects.

Keep your eyes on Jesus so that He might manifest Himself in the midst of your mess. Yes, that may mean some difficult days up ahead, but if you will keep going, you will make it through. Remember, you don't walk this road alone.

CHAPTER 3

The Greatness
of Grace

Many women own pearl necklaces. My wife, Lois, had a number of pearl necklaces that she loved to wear. Pearls are beautiful and can be fairly expensive. But did you know that the precious pearls, which adorn the necks of so many women in the world, were all born out of affliction? They were produced by pain. While they may look nice now, if you or I could have seen them when they were being constructed, we would have seen something messy and altogether different from the finished jewelry.

While much mystery remains around exactly how pearls are made, we do know a few things. First of all, they come from oysters. From what we can understand, the oyster in which the pearl is formed first has something foreign enter into its world—something unplanned, unanticipated, and uninvited makes its way inside its shell, creating an irritation. It could be a grain of sand or even an insect of some kind. Whatever it is that makes its way in, it irritates the oyster considerably.

Because the oyster is not able to remove the irritation from within, it has been designed with a way to cope with it instead. This takes place through the increased secretion of nacre. Nacre is an organic composite material that naturally lines the inner shell of oysters and some others in the mollusk family. On its own the nacre is not considered valuable. But when the nacre begins to surround a grain of sand or grit, it develops into a pearl. Each pearl is formed out of protection. It is formed out of a need to soothe pain. The iridescent coating that is secreted helps the oyster live with that which it could never get rid of on its own.

Out of that problem comes a pearl. The pearl didn't start out as a pearl. The pearl started out as an irritant. It started out as something entirely unwelcomed, undesired, and unexpected. Yet since the oyster could not rid itself of it, the pure mess of the irritation transformed into a magnificent miracle known as the mother-of-pearl.

You can probably see where I'm going here. Because when you are in the middle of something causing you pain and hurt, it's easy to fixate on the problem. But if you will learn how to cope with the problem, using the tools God has endowed you with, you can participate in the birthing of beauty from within.

Paul speaks to this type of transformation in 2 Corinthians 12. He introduces the concept in verse 7, where he writes: "Because of the surpassing greatness of the revelations, for this reason, to keep me from exalting myself, there was given me a thorn in the flesh, a messenger of Satan to torment me—to keep me from exalting myself!"

Paul refers to that which was causing him pain as a thorn. He calls it a "thorn in the flesh." Sounds very similar to the grit or grain of sand inside of the oyster. The Greek word for *thorn* can be translated "splinter." Have you ever had a splinter in your skin that you just couldn't pull out? If you chose to leave it there rather than dig it out, your skin would soon turn red and tender around it. The irritation of the splinter would nag you and nag you and nag you until you did something about it.

The "thorn in the flesh" that Paul speaks of is also a nagging irritation. He isn't talking about something he could choose to ignore. The thorn in the flesh must be dealt with and addressed in some form or fashion, even if that simply means learning how to cope with the hurt it has caused. Just like the oyster.

I'll never forget the time I had an ingrown toenail. If you've had one before, then you know why I can't forget it. When a person's toenail grows up and around in order to dig itself into their skin, the irritation it produces becomes too much to bear. Each step on that foot causes indescribable pain.

Another irritant you may have experienced physically is a toothache. A toothache caused by bacteria deep within your gums can produce a throbbing pain that simply won't stop without an intervention. You may try to get rid of it yourself. You may even try to solve it with some over-the-counter medication, but all you've done is delay the problem for a later time. Unless you allow a professional to get to the root of the pain in the tooth, the pain will continue to flare up in such a way and to such a degree that it can shut you down.

I had this kind of pain when Lois and I had gone on a cruise overseas. The pain was so bad that all I could do was sit in our cabin and nurse it through medication or hot rags placed on my jaw. I couldn't enjoy the scenery. I couldn't enjoy the food. I couldn't do any of the things we had planned to do—even catch up on reading and rest—because of the pain of this one tooth. It wasn't until I called my dentist back in the States and he prescribed me an antibiotic and prescription pain medication that I was able to spend a few remaining days on the cruise without such a degree of pain.

Paul knew about pain when he spoke of this "thorn in the flesh." Whatever it was he faced, he knew the struggle and difficulties pain can produce. After all, he lived at a time when there weren't often quick fixes to alleviate pain. A "thorn in the flesh," whatever it was, could knock a person out of his or her ability to function. It could leave someone flat on their back.

While Paul doesn't tell us what the pain was, he does tell us the root. He refers to his pain as a "messenger of Satan" sent to "torment" him. In many ways it is more helpful to us, as readers of Scripture, to not know what the thorn was, because then we can identify with what it caused, even if we don't identify with what it was. You, as you study Scripture, can insert your personal thorn, or thorns, into this text. You can put your emotional, relational, financial, or physical thorn—whether it stems from a particular person, other people, problems, or literal physical pain—into the context of this passage in order to discover how to address it.

I imagine if you picked up this book to read, you have a thorn in the flesh somewhere, somehow. The reason you know it's a thorn is because it hurts and you can't get rid of it. You can't shake it. You can't remove the impact of it on your peace or ability to function. In fact, I imagine you have even prayed about it. Paul did. He tells us he prayed repeatedly. We read in verse 8: "Concerning this I implored the Lord three times that it might leave me." Paul asked God to do something about his pain and his hurt. He implored God to get rid of it. But even though he asked again and again, it didn't get any better. His painful situation only continued.

This brings me to a point I've mentioned before but want to be sure and emphasize again because it is a truth we often forget. Paul was a very spiritual person who sought after the heart and plan of God. Yet, even though he dedicated his life to God, he experienced great hardship and pain. One principle we can obtain from this is that thorns, difficulties, and negative realities come even to the most spiritual people. And since that is the case, we need to find out why.

Paul answers this question for us in the verse we just looked at earlier, verse 7. He began the verse by saying, "Because of the surpassing greatness of the revelations, for this reason, to keep me from exalting myself." Paul tells us why he had to experience the hurt which he did. It was due to his anointing. It came about because of the revelations he experienced. Paul's divinely ordained purpose required that he experience a thorn.

> Thorns, difficulties, and negative realities come even to the most spiritual people.

Take a quick glance at 2 Corinthians 12:1–6 and you'll see that Paul is the only person, outside of Jesus Himself, who got to go to the third heaven and come back from it. God exposed the apostle Paul to things no one else had previously been exposed to. This experience overwhelmed him. He couldn't even find the right words to describe it in full.

And while Paul was no doubt humbled by the extraordinary experience of visiting the third heaven, he was also now in a tempting position of thinking more highly of himself as well. After all, he had been given a glimpse that no other human had. Now, we already know that Paul had a propensity toward pride before this experience. He was a spiritual man, but he wasn't perfect. He could get the big head if he spent too much time thinking about his pedigree, history, and calling. So this additional visit to the third heaven no doubt would have pushed him over the edge. That's why he tells us this thorn was given, in order to "keep me from exalting myself" (v. 7). Paul had to be kept humble, and pain is one of the ways God does that.

The more blessed, useful, and influential you become, the more prideful you are likely to be. That's the way our flesh works. God used this thorn in Paul's life in order to deflate him. God wanted to strip him of his pride.

A lady came to her pastor one day and said, "Pastor, I'm struggling. I really need you to pray for me." The pastor responded by saying he would be happy to pray for her and asked what her prayer need was about. She responded, "Whenever I come to church and look around, I struggle with pride because I'm the prettiest one here."

The pastor took a deep breath and then replied, "Well, ma'am, that's not only a sin but also a mistake."

Pride has a way of blinding the person who has it. I'm sure you know the Scripture that says, "Pride goes before destruction, and a haughty spirit before stumbling" (Prov. 16:18). Some translations say it like this: "Pride goes before the fall."

This reminds me of the frog who had to cross the lake, but he didn't have anything to jump on in order to get across on his own. After some searching, the frog came across two birds. The frog asked the birds if they would help him cross the lake. The birds agreed, and the frog shared his ingenious plan for them to do just that.

After telling of the plan, one of the birds flew off to get the fairly long stick, which the frog said was needed. Then, when the bird flew back, the other bird picked up the end of the stick in its mouth as well. The birds then waited until the frog got in the middle of the stick and grabbed the middle with his mouth. Once everyone was holding on tightly, the birds took off flying.

The problem came about midway over the lake when another bird saw what they were doing and asked who had come up with such an ingenious idea. That's when the frog opened his big mouth to say, "I did!"

Pride definitely comes before the fall, or drop, in the case of this frog. God allows thorns into our lives in order to deal with both actual and potential sins. Thus, if there is something nagging you that you just can't seem to get rid of, and even God won't remove it when you ask Him, look for the principle in the pain.

As Paul mentioned, his thorn was" a messenger of Satan." It had been sent to cause him "torment" (2 Cor. 12:7). But what you and I must always remember about the devil is that the devil is not some equal and opposite power of God. Sometimes we think of the world as an evenly matched battle between good and bad, and we're waiting to see how things turn out. That's not the case at all. God has the devil on a leash.

If your thorn is being precipitated by the devil, then it means that God is simultaneously allowing it. In other words, God is letting the devil mess with you on purpose. And what the devil means for evil, God means for good.

After all, isn't that what He did with Job? It was God who pointed out Job to Satan. Job 1:8 reveals a chilling truth: "The LORD said to Satan, 'Have you considered My servant Job? For there is no one like him on the earth, a blameless and upright man, fearing God and turning away from evil.'"

God literally told Satan to take a closer look at Job. He put him on Satan's radar. He did the same for His Son Jesus Christ when we read in Matthew 4:1: "Then Jesus was led up by the Spirit into the wilderness to be tempted by the devil." The Holy Spirit led Jesus straight into the devil's land to tempt Him. To blame the devil for any or all problems you face is to dismiss the reality that God is sovereign. Nothing comes to you that does not first pass through His fingers.

If you truly want to know how to cope with the pain and hurt in your life, then you need to turn to

God and ask Him why He has allowed it. You need to discern from Him what it is He is wanting you to use as a tool to cope with it. He may or may not remove it. But you have a choice on how you respond to it.

In Paul's case, the reason for the thorn was explained clearly when God told him why it was there. We read what Paul has to say in 2 Corinthians 12:9 where it says, "And He has said to me, 'My grace is sufficient for you, for power is perfected in weakness.' Most gladly, therefore, I will rather boast about my weaknesses, so that the power of Christ may dwell in me."

God told Paul that His grace was sufficient for him. He explained that spiritual power becomes perfected through weakness. He didn't remove the thorn. He didn't even heal the hurt. The torment remained just like the grain of sand or grit inside an oyster. But what God did do is reveal to Paul the path forward through the pain. Like the oyster coating the sand with nacre, God told Paul to coat his thorn with God's grace.

> Spiritual power becomes perfected through weakness.

Grace is God's divine provision He delegates to us in order to meet a need. Grace is the favor God bestows upon us, favor that is undeserved. Grace is God giving us what we cannot earn, cannot pay for, and could not do for ourselves. In short, grace is the inexhaustible supply of God's goodness. And while we often want the thorns of life pulled out and the pain to cease altogether, God says there are times and seasons when grace to get through it is going to reveal the sufficiency of His power within us.

The word *grace* is a term many of us use, but few have truly maximized. Sure, we've experienced grace in salvation, but we miss out on the power of grace in our everyday lives. Second Corinthians 9:8 is the

> Grace is the inexhaustible supply of God's goodness.

single greatest verse on the subject of grace in all of Scripture. I'd encourage you to memorize it and apply it to your life, especially when times are tough. It says, "And God is able to make all grace abound to you, so that always having all sufficiency in everything, you may have an abundance for every good deed."

Read that again. Write it down on a piece of paper and stick it somewhere you will see it often. Memorize it. And as you do, pay attention to the word *all*. God has so much grace to give you that you will have enough for all you face. In fact, He says in this verse that you will have an abundance of grace—enough to supply what you need for every good thing you choose to think, say, or do. God will never run out of grace. He has enough for you. He has enough for me. And I can share with you personally that when life gets tough and you don't know how you will bear it on your own, God's grace gives you the power to make it through.

Thorns, when accompanied by God's grace, are designed to work for us, not against us. In this way, the thorn literally becomes an asset even though it once felt like a liability. Once you mix that thorn with God's grace, that grain of sand becomes a priceless pearl. The thing you thought was driving you crazy actually begins to produce something within you of inestimable value. But grace won't produce its intended result if you choose to focus on the thorn rather than on what God has given you to coat it. If you try to dig out that thorn yourself because you don't want to learn how to cope with the pain or live with the hurt, then you will only create more cuts, which can lead to infections.

Mixing grace with your pain produces power. It perfects your spiritual power. It activates the power of God's Spirit in you.

Some of you have Extra Strength Tylenol in your medicine cabinets. Now, I don't know about you, but I only take Extra Strength Tylenol when I have a problem. I don't just go into the medicine cabinet every single day and take some when I'm feeling fine. But if I have a headache I can't seem to shake, I know what to take to get rid of it. What takes me to the power of the Tylenol is the pain. It's the weakness that comes about due to a throbbing headache. In the pill called Tylenol is the power to address the problem, but I wouldn't take one without the problem in the first place.

The reason God hasn't gotten rid of a lot of the problems we face and a lot of the hurt we experience is because He wants us to reach for His grace. He wants us to grab hold of His grace. He wants us to access the power in His grace which is perfected in our weaknesses. If there is no weakness, you don't get to see the power. Paul understood this. He knew it firsthand. That's why he told us, as we saw earlier, that he would rather boast in his weaknesses so that the power of Jesus Christ would be made even greater within him (2 Cor. 12:9). In fact, he went on to emphasize this truth by stating it again, in another way: "Therefore I am well content with weaknesses, with insults, with distresses, with persecutions, with difficulties, for Christ's sake; for when I am weak, then I am strong" (v. 10).

Paul let us know that he would remain content with whatever was causing his weakness. He would choose to do the opposite of what we normally do in our humanity. Rather than complain about it, he would boast about it. Rather than allow it to keep him down, he would rise up in the strength and power it produced. Paul knew that in his weakness he was truly strong.

Now, keep in mind, Paul isn't sugarcoating his hurt. He isn't acting like it doesn't exist. He's not posting photos of only smiles and sunny days. He's calling the spade a spade. He's acknowledging the insults, distresses, persecutions, and difficulties. But in his acknowledgment and awareness of what is happening to him, he's remembering the power of God. He's recalling what he saw in the third heaven. He's focusing on the grace from a greater Source than anything he could produce on his own. He's keeping an eternal perspective in his temporal pain.

Through this approach and the tools of accessing grace, Paul chooses to rest and remain content in spite of his circumstances. You and I can choose to do the same. It comes about through a decision you make on where to focus. Are you going to focus on trying to rid yourself of the pain you've experienced, or are you going to coat it with the soothing ointment of God's grace?

A great Old Testament illustration of this is the man named Jacob. Jacob was often up to no good. He was the deceiver who enjoyed tricking people. On one occasion, he found himself between a rock and hard place. Esau, his twin brother whom he had deceived and robbed, was coming with a bunch of men to kill Jacob. Jacob had no real way to escape. He was in a bad situation, a desperate scenario. His life was literally on the line.

Then, out of nowhere, the angel of the Lord showed up. But the angel of the Lord didn't show up to immediately save the day. Instead, the angel wrestled with Jacob throughout the night, making Jacob's bad situation seem even more disastrous.

Yet all night long, as Jacob went without the sleep he desperately needed in order to navigate the upcoming battle he faced, he wouldn't give up. He kept wrestling the angel. He kept hanging on to the hope of victory. He kept the faith and kept the fight. Finally, near daybreak, when the angel asked Jacob to let him go, Jacob said he would only do so if the angel blessed him. He laid down terms. The angel of the Lord then took his finger and touched the socket in Jacob's thigh in order to dislocate it, totally removing Jacob's ability to wrestle.

Yet Jacob hung on. As his pain grew in intensity and as his own power declined, he hung on to the hope that the angel would bless him. He remained firm in his faith. He remained convinced that even though he may not deserve a blessing, God could give him a blessing because he chose to believe and to ask. Finally, the angel of the Lord rewarded Jacob's heart and blessed him. He told him from that day on, he would no longer be known as Jacob the deceiver. His new name would be Israel (Gen. 32:24–32).

In changing Jacob's name, God was changing his destiny. A name in biblical culture meant more than just a name. It was an indicator of character, calling, and the covenant. Jacob's pain brought him to a place where he received his purpose. Sure, his world had to fall apart before it could happen. He had to experience disappointment after disappointment after disappointment. But eventually God gave Jacob the grace he needed to move forward in a greater calling and anointed character in covenant relationship with God.

That's not to say Jacob's future was pain free. We know it wasn't. From that point on, Jacob walked with a limp and used a cane. Instead of walking in the firmness of his own strength, which had been his lifestyle, he had to hobble in the weakness of his infirmities. But lest you look upon Jacob with any amount of pity, just know that—like Paul—Jacob wouldn't have traded his limp (thorn) for anything. In fact, he'd quickly remind anyone who would listen that his limp is a good limp. It's a special limp. It's a grace limp. He'd tell us all that every time he took a step, he was reminded of the day God broke him and then blessed him and then changed his future forever.

I don't know what your thorn is or the hurt that clouds your heart. But I want you to know that there is a grace that will enable you to experience goodness again. There is a grace that will provide purpose for your pain. If you will just cling to God, wrestle with Him through prayer, fasting, and obedience to His Word, you will find the blessing in the brokenness He's allowed you to experience. You can be content in spite of your circumstances. You can know power in spite of your problems. All of this is available to you when you choose to accept the grace of God in the midst of the grit and the grime that show up in your life. "[His] grace is sufficient for you" (2 Cor. 12:9). It's there for the taking.

The choice to end up with a priceless pearl or a dirty piece of sand is entirely up to you. You get to decide how you respond to life's thorns.

CHAPTER 4

Healing through Humility

In Luke 8, we read about a woman who suffered from an illness for twelve years. It was an illness that had to do with her blood. She had a hemorrhage that could not be healed by anyone. If you look at how it is described in the King James Version, it is called "an issue of blood" (v. 43).

Now, if you are bleeding, your life is ebbing away because the life of the flesh is in the blood. You may have heard the term *bleeding out*, when some people die in an accident or from other things. Bleeding out takes place when your body loses enough blood that you no longer have enough to sustain you. What the body needs to live, have strength, and survive is in the blood. Blood is a critical component of life.

When a person suffers from cancer or other life-threatening diseases, one of the biggest concerns as the disease progresses can be the loss of blood due to internal hemorrhaging. To compensate for this, the patient will often routinely get blood transfusions. He or she will receive fresh blood into their body so that they have the strength to fight another day.

The lady we are going to look at in this chapter, as we examine how to access hope while we are hurting, suffered from an issue of blood. As a result, she probably lacked strength. She may have lacked mental clarity. Her life was ebbing away from her. Certainly, her physical life was ebbing away, but other aspects of her life were ebbing away too. When you lose enough blood, you no longer have the right amount of oxygen flowing through the various parts of your body. As a result, the other parts of your body—including your brain—are going to suffer decay as well.

Yet not only was her physical life fading, her financial life had taken a hit as well. Over the course of these twelve years as she suffered, she had spent all she had on doctors and medication. Mark, in his telling of the story, puts it like this: "A woman who had had a hemorrhage for twelve years, and had endured much at the hands of many physicians, and had spent all that she had and was not helped at all, but rather had grown worse" (Mark 5:25–26).

Not only had her illness diminished her capacity and function in her body, but it had eroded her bank account. She had doctor bills she could not pay because of a problem they could not fix. But not only were her physical and financial life suffering ravaging attacks, her spiritual life had suffered as well. We know this to be the case because, according to Leviticus 15:25, she would be classified as "unclean." The Scripture summarizes her issue in this way: "Now if a woman has a discharge of her blood many days, not at the period of her menstrual impurity, or if she has a discharge beyond that period, all the days of her impure discharge she shall continue as though in her menstrual impurity; she is unclean."

If a person was considered to be "unclean" in those days, the person could not be touched. She could not enter the temple to worship God. She was an outcast.

So not only did she have to face a life of physical, financial, and spiritual pain, she also grew weary as a social outcast. She was alone, trying to survive, without much hope at all.

A few years ago, this woman's story may have seemed distant to us. It may have felt like a narrative no one could identify with, in our country at least, in any shape or form. But with the onset of the pandemic—which led to a significant amount of isolation and quarantining for countless people—this woman's story may have begun feeling more relevant than ever before. Many families experienced what it was like to have a loved one fall sick, only to be unable to visit this loved one at all. Many more were prohibited from physically checking in on their elderly relatives in nursing homes or long-term care facilities. If you fell sick yourself, then you know what being sick in isolation felt like. People may have dropped off medication or food to your door, but the lack of personal comfort that comes through human interaction took a toll. As a result, emotional and spiritual issues increased just as much as, if not more than, physical issues.

Even if you did not personally become sick, you still can relate to the issue of life closing down all around you. It could have come through a limitation of social engagement, financial opportunity, physical freedom, or even spiritual nourishment as churches had to pause in-person gatherings.

This woman we read about in Luke 8 doesn't seem so far-fetched to many of us anymore. We can identify more fully with what Luke says when he describes her as someone who "could not be healed by anyone" (v. 43). In other words, there was no human resource available to her any longer to even attempt to fix her. All of the professionals, all of the contacts, all of the family, all of the relationships, all of the spiritual leaders that had been designed to address and rectify issues in others' lives were unable to help her. She sat alone, desperate, in an unfixable scenario—at least from a human point of view.

But she still had hope.

Before we see how her faith took shape, I want to remind you that if you are dealing with an issue in your life where you are aching, discouraged, despondent, and disappointed, you should not give up. Even though there seems to be no human solution to the trial you face, God has a way of setting the captives free. Jesus has a way of reversing that which seems irreversible. It may mean transferring your focus from human solutions to God alone, but if it will get you healed and restore the life flow within you, isn't it worth it to try?

The lady we read about in Luke 8 had run out of options. She had lost all hope from a worldly perspective. But that's when she heard about this man named Jesus who was coming to her town.

Jesus was on His way to the house of man named Jairus. Jairus had asked Jesus to come to his home in order to heal his daughter, but before Jesus could get there, this woman came to Him. Now, if you are familiar with the story, you know she didn't come to Him the normal way people do. She didn't introduce herself or shake His hand. She didn't start a conversation. Rather, she did all she could do with the strength that she had. She came up behind him—low to the ground, presumably, due to her lack of energy from the loss of blood—and she touched the fringe of the clothes He had on.

Luke's rendering of her story tells us that when she touched His garment, she was immediately healed. Her hemorrhaging stopped (v. 44). The thing she could not get rid of for twelve long years had been dealt with instantly by Christ. The thing that had dominated all her thoughts, her money, her way of life for more than a decade suddenly came to a close with one swift touch of Christ's cloak.

That must have been some garment! But, if we look closer at her story by reading what Matthew had to say, we will discover that it wasn't the garment that did it. Matthew 9:20–21 describes what happened like this: "And a woman who had been suffering from a hemorrhage for twelve years, came up behind Him and touched the fringe of His cloak; for she was saying to herself, 'If I only touch His garment, I will get well.'"

She was talking to herself. She was encouraging herself. Despite her isolation and the rest of the entire world known to her at that point having given up on her, she had not yet given up herself. She clung to what she believed like there was no tomorrow.

No doubt she had heard about the miracles of this man named Jesus. Perhaps she had even seen people who had been healed. When all hope should have been gone, the flicker of hope inside of her burst into a flame when she heard about Jesus and what He could do.

In this situation, we can see how influential testimonies of life change can be. Jesus' reputation as someone who could heal spread near and far because those whose lives had been impacted by Him were willing to talk about it. They didn't keep their blessing to themselves. They didn't hide their joy or bask alone in their newfound hope. They talked about it. They shared what He did with others. They gave witness to the power of Jesus Christ. As a result, this woman's faith and, consequently, her hope revived.

If she could only touch the hem of His garment, she knew she would be healed. But why the hem? The book of Numbers will help us understand her thinking. God spoke to Moses concerning the hems of the garments of the Israelite men, giving instructions to them to place a symbolic reminder on what they wore each day. It is recorded in Numbers 15:37–40 like this:

> The LORD also spoke to Moses, saying, "Speak
> to the sons of Israel, and tell them that they
> shall make for themselves tassels on the cor-
> ners of their garments throughout their gen-
> erations, and that they shall put on the tassel
> of each corner a cord of blue. It shall be a tassel

for you to look at and remember all the commandments of the LORD, so as to do them and not follow after your own heart and your own eyes, after which you played the harlot, so that you may remember to do all My commandments and be holy to your God."

These tassels were to remind the Israelites of God's Word—His expectations, commandments, and rule. The woman suffering from an issue of blood knew this. She knew the significance of the hem where the tassels hung. She believed that if she could grab hold of the hem, for even a moment in time, she would access the power of God and His Word through the One she had heard so much about—Jesus. She was reaching for that which she knew could heal her.

Keep in mind, to reach for the hem of a garment, a person needs to go low. The hem and the tassels were at the bottom of what Jesus had on. In order to grab it, she had to bend down. She had to kneel. She had to place herself in a posture of humility. Don't skip over that reality in this story, because pride is one of the greatest hindrances to finding hope in hard times. If you are so proud that you are not willing to get low enough to touch the hem or the tassel, then you are still operating from the mindset that you can work this thing out on your own. God will not compete with you in order to heal you. He doesn't mix His power with yours. If you choose to rely on yourself, He will wait until you come to the end of yourself and know that it is God, and God alone, who has the power you need to find the hope you have lost.

As we saw in Numbers 15, the tassels were a reminder of God's Word. God's Word is a revelation of His heart, His way, and His rule. It is God's path that produces healing. It is God's ways that restore health and hope. We often quote Proverbs 3:5–6 by memory, but how many of us have gone on to read what turning to God, His Word, and His ways will produce in our lives? The next few verses are revealing, especially in light of the context of this woman's story: "Trust in the LORD with all your heart and do not lean on your own understanding. In all your ways acknowledge Him, and He

> Pride is one of the greatest hindrances to finding hope in hard times.

will make your paths straight. Do not be wise in your own eyes; fear the LORD and turn away from evil. It will be healing to your body and refreshment to your bones" (Prov. 3:5–8).

The "evil" we are to turn from as indicated in this passage—first and foremost—is pride. We are not to be wise in our own eyes. The quickest way to locate hope for the hurt you face is letting go of "your own understanding" and turning to God and His Word. Let go of your perspective. Release what you see or don't see but are desperately trying to figure out. Suspend your logic for a spell in order to gain a clearer spiritual perspective. Don't fixate on what you can figure out or what you can't. Rather, grab the hem of the garment. Grab the tassel of Christ, which is the Word of God, made manifest as the living Word Himself.

Look to Jesus for the solution in whatever situation you face. In Him is summed up all of the law and the prophets (Matt. 22:40) because He is the living Word (John 1:1–5). Your hope is not to be found in your own analysis of what is going on in your life, your situation, or even in the country and our world right now. Your hope is to be found in Jesus Christ. Look here, not there. Don't let the devil distract you.

The woman expressed a statement of faith that when she connected to the Word of God through the Son of God, she would be made well. She believed in Jesus' power, based on the Word, to change her situation. She knew He could fix what she could never fix herself.

If you are in a similar situation of hopelessness as this woman, I just want to know one thing: Have you reached for the hem yet? Have you humbled yourself to grab hold of the tassels of truth? The problem far too many people find themselves handicapped by is that as long as you think you have human options for your solutions, you will never kneel to access the power you need. The reason why a lot of us aren't better from whatever it is that ails us, cripples us, or keeps us knocked down is that we haven't run out of our own ways yet. We haven't run out of money. We haven't run out of connections. We haven't run out of doctors, medication, self-help books, or any of the rest of the things we turn to in place of Jesus Himself.

We remain in a continual flow of hemorrhaging our strength, resources, and even our health and hope when we can't stop the bleeding of pride. We can't clamp down on the bleeding of human wisdom. We can't control the bleeding of personal power. Please know that God will allow you to run out of human options if you continue to insist on pursuing them rather than pursuing Him. This woman had nothing else to look toward for her healing and hope. When she had finally run out of all her own methods and strategies to restore her life, she knelt down low enough to touch the hem of the One whose power makes all things well.

When we experience the living Word, Jesus Christ, through the written Word, we are experiencing the operative power of the Word itself. The two work together. If you go to the written Word but leave out the living Word—an abiding relationship with Jesus—you will have truth but no life. Or, if you go to the living Word only at the exclusion of the written Word, you access life with no understanding of how to apply it to your daily decisions and needs. It is when you combine the written Word, symbolized by the tassels on the hem of Jesus' garment, with intimate fellowship with the living Word—Jesus Himself—that you have life, wisdom, healing, and truth. As Jesus said, "I came that they may have life, and have it abundantly" (John 10:10).

Healing and hope don't have to take long to reach you when you combine the written Word with the living Word. As we see in our story of the woman struggling with an issue of blood, she got her miracle immediately. Luke 8:44 makes a point of telling us this: "[She] came up behind Him and touched the fringe of His cloak, and immediately her hemorrhage stopped."

Immediately. Last I checked, *immediately* means "pretty quick."

How would you like to have whatever it is that is causing you pain and suffering be removed or fixed immediately in your life? I think we all would. But that's exactly what Jesus can do when we go to Him according to His prescribed ways, trusting in His unlimited power and grace. He doesn't always do this for us. Sometimes, like Paul, we live with the thorn; or like Jacob, we walk with the limp. But sometimes He makes the problem go away on the spot.

Sometimes it seems that we try too hard. We complicate things. We make things more difficult than they should be. We do this because a simple solution of turning to Jesus with our whole hearts seems too . . . simple. Touching the hem of His garment seems too easy. Too inexpensive. Too quick. At times it seems more difficult to believe in God's pathway to miracles than it does to believe in our own complex plans. Jesus said if we will just speak to the mountain in faith, it will move. Not only that, He tells us we can lift the mountain and toss it into the sea with our faith (Mark 11:23). Keep in mind, in biblical texts, mountains often refer to the impossible troubles people face, difficulties piling up in their path.

But instead of speaking to the mountains of our lives, we invest in bulldozers. We spend hours learning how to drive them. We seek our own solutions when the miracle of moving the mountain is in our own mouths. Just speak to it, Jesus says. It will move. Or, as in the story of the woman with the issue of blood, just touch the tassels and you will be healed. Power is accessed when Christ is pursued based on His written Word.

> Power is accessed when Christ is pursued based on His written Word.

In fact, Jesus could feel the power the woman accessed through her faith. Faith is that strong. When the hem of His robe was touched, He sensed His power leave Him for her, and so He asked: "Who is the one who touched Me?" (Luke 8:45a).

The disciples were confused by His question. The area was crowded to begin with, and people had a habit of standing in close proximity to the Savior. Peter spoke up first among them: "Peter said, 'Master, the people are crowding and pressing in on You.' But Jesus said, 'Someone did touch Me, for I was aware that power had gone out of Me'" (vv. 45b–46).

Jesus was aware of the power that had left Him. But what's more is that He was also surrounded by a large crowd of people when it happened. His power didn't leave Him generically to be accessed by everyone. His healing power went directly to the woman with humble faith. The principle we can glean from this is that you can be part of the crowd and not have Jesus release His power to you. You can even rub up against Jesus and still not get His power. He isn't a lucky charm. Being in the Jesus vicinity doesn't equate to miracles in your life. Attending church doesn't pull down the power of Jesus into your situation. Going to Bible studies doesn't do it either. Even if you choose to be part of the Jesus Fan Club, that doesn't guarantee you His power.

The fundamental difference between the woman who got healed and the many others surrounding Jesus at that time was faith. Her faith became manifest through her actions. She humbled herself, in belief, to carry out an action she thought would bring her healing. She went low in order to rise high in hope. She knelt down in order to regain her strength to stand tall once again.

The others around Jesus were simply part of a crowd. They placed themselves on the same level as Jesus. They didn't bow in reverence. They didn't commit to actions of faith demonstrating their belief in Him. They merely hung out with Him. In return, they got what they asked for—an opportunity to hang out with Him. And while that's nice, most often it is not enough.

In this life, most of us face real problems which challenge our hearts and try our souls. Hanging out with Jesus isn't enough to cope with sudden loss, or the death of a dream, or even your own physical ailments. You and I need His healing power. We need to access His miraculous mercy so that our hope can be returned and our spirits can soar in His grace.

Another important thing to point out about how this woman approached Jesus is that she did not approach him in a way that showcased herself. Essentially, she hid where most people would not be looking. She didn't make her miracle or her encounter all about her.

I know we live in a day where social media has opened the floodgates for egoistic spirituality to flourish. We must be cautious of not wearing our perceived spirituality as a badge. The woman who received the miracle didn't use a filter on her photo. She didn't turn her experience into a twenty-one-day journey for others to join, in order to sell them something at the end. She didn't seek her own followers so she could start running ads on her account. No, she knelt down and touched Jesus' hem for herself. And based on Jesus' response, she was content to leave it at that.

Once she received the power of her healing, she didn't stand up and introduce herself to Him. We know that she knew she had been healed because Mark tells us that in his account of the story. He says, "she felt in her body that she was healed of her affliction" (Mark 5:29).

This woman didn't seek to parlay the power she had received into further personal gain. In fact, Jesus had to inquire as to who had touched Him. He had to look for her.

Why do you think Jesus looked for her? Is it because He truly did not know who had touched Him? Or do you think it could have been to draw attention to her faith? I lean toward the latter. As God, Jesus would have known who touched Him. He also knew the level of humility she had shown alongside the level of faith she had in Him. By pointing her out to the others, and to all of us as we read her story in the Gospels, He was using her faith as an example for our own. Jesus was inviting her to testify of what He had done for her.

It's amazing how many people want to testify in order to create their own spiritual persona, even though they have never truly been touched by the power of God. At the same time, so many who do receive His power and His miracles in their life have to be encouraged to speak on it. In a way, their reverence for Christ may inhibit them from speaking out. But Jesus knows how important it is for those who have experienced His power to share it with others. That's why He sought the woman out. Her response reveals her own fear and timidity He was aiming to overcome. We read in Mark 5:33: "But the woman fearing and trembling, aware of what had happened to her, came and fell down before Him and told Him the whole truth."

Once encouraged by Jesus, she didn't hold back. She spoke up and shared the whole story of what had happened to her. She not only received healing on that day, but she received a quiet boldness enabling her to testify of His grace throughout the remainder of her time on earth. Jesus' response to her and her willingness to tell about what had happened reveals a lot. We read it in Luke 8:48: "And He said to her, 'Daughter, your faith has made you well; go in peace.'"

What started as a situation of a lonely and abandoned woman suffering with an issue of blood ends with Jesus calling her by the term of endearment, "Daughter." Somehow between getting physically healed and telling her story, she established a relationship with the Lord. She became as a daughter to Him. She entered into something beyond a physical blessing. She became part of the family of God.

Unfortunately, today, far too many people want healing for their hurts but not a relationship with the Healer. They come to church to show God they are being faithful so that He will give them a new car, a better marriage, or any number of things. In short, they come with the intention that they will get blessed somehow. But they aren't interested in the rest of the story. They aren't interested in spending time with Jesus, just talking. They aren't interested in opening up to Him and experiencing the calming power of His presence.

> Too many people want healing for their hurts but not a relationship with the Healer.

It's fascinating to me to note how even though the Scripture tells us that the woman's bleeding stopped when she touched the hem of Christ's robe, it does not call her "well" until after she spoke with Him herself. It wasn't until after she spent time with Christ and opened up her heart to Him that He said she had been made well. See, God can bless you with things that you can touch, see, or enjoy, while somehow you are still not entirely "well." It isn't until you establish a close, abiding relationship with Jesus that wholeness happens and hope returns.

Jesus wants to do more for you than just heal you. He wants to do more for you than just fix the things in your life that are broken. He wants to do more for you than miracles. He wants to do more than just relieve you of your suffering. He wants you to be whole. Jesus wants you to be well. He wants you to know what it means to have close personal fellowship with Him. He desires that you enter into a deeper intimacy with Him. This takes place when you willingly reach out for God's Word while also reaching out for His Son, Jesus Christ. When you look to the power of God's living and written Word together, and they begin to sync up in your life, you will access power like no other—but this requires humbling yourself.

Look to Jesus when you are at your lowest. Look to Him when you have nowhere else to go. He is waiting for you to reach out to Him in faith so that He can unleash a torrent of hope within your soul.

CHAPTER 5

Come Get Your Rest

The *Pelicano* was one of the most unwanted ships in the world. In 1986, there was a sanitation strike in the city of Philadelphia, coming right after the Democratic Convention. Myriads of people left myriads of trash that was uncollected and unaddressed. Since the sanitation workers had gone on strike, the trash became a health hazard to the city. That's when the ship named the *Pelicano* was brought in. It was a freighter. Nearly thirty tons of trash, some of it burned and fuming with toxic ash, were placed on board.

Because the trash had become so toxic, the *Pelicano* had nowhere to go. No country would allow it to dock because no nation wanted to allow the toxic waste into their space. So for two years, the *Pelicano* floated on the sea looking for a place to rest. The only permissions it was granted over that time were to stop and refuel so it could go back on its way.

A lot of us are like this *Pelicano* in more ways than we might even know. Life can heap garbage and trash upon us until it accumulates into something toxic. Sure, we may go to church with hopes of ridding it— only to discover that all we can do is refuel enough to make it through another week. We leave church carrying the same heavy weight we had when we walked in.

Toxic trash in our lives can come in many forms. It mainly shows up when hurt and pain are allowed to fester, just as when any wound is left untreated, bacteria will accumulate and ooze nasty puss. The deeper the wound, the more damaging it is when left unaddressed. Bacteria in our soul produces bitterness, hate, rage, judgment, blame, low self-worth, apathy, anger, and more. Bacteria takes our hurts and turns them into sins, which do even greater damage than the original hurt ever did before.

That's why it is so important to seek healing for your hurt and hope for your heart. One of Satan's most effective strategies is tempting us to sin through the weakness we face when we are suffering. That's why Scripture says: "Be angry, and yet do not sin; do not let the sun go down on your anger, and do not give the devil an opportunity" (Eph. 4:26–27). The devil gets an opportunity when you hold on to your hurt. When you nurse your pain. When you pout over the things that cause you to feel angry. Satan loves it when you do this because you open the door for him to walk right in and declare a stronghold on your spirit and emotions.

The Path to Healing

The path to healing from hurt and hope for your heart is in letting go of the difficulties, pains, injustices, disappointments, and all else that has legitimately or illegitimately—through your own fault or through no fault of your own—caused you pain. Saying that and doing it are two entirely different things; I realize that. But Jesus wants to offer you a place to dock. He wants to give you a place to not only refuel but release the load you are burdened with. We discover how to do that in Matthew 11.

He begins what He has to say with a prayer. In verses 25–27, we read Jesus' prayer: "At that time Jesus said, 'I praise You, Father, Lord of heaven and earth, that You have hidden these things from the wise and intelligent and have revealed them to infants. Yes, Father, for this way was well-pleasing in Your sight. All things have been handed over to Me by My Father; and no one knows the Son except the Father; nor does anyone know the Father except the Son, and anyone to whom the Son wills to reveal Him.'"

Notice that Jesus is getting ready to tell us how to release the burden. He's preparing to tell us how to get rid of the garbage in order to find comfort in affliction. But before He does, He starts with a prayer. He reminds those who were listening, and those who are reading today, that the hope to comfort your hurt does not get discovered in the ivory-tower institutions of our land. Information without illumination means little. Those who consider themselves "wise and intelligent" according to the world's ways are fools in the kingdom of God. God's kingdom doesn't operate according to the agenda of this world. His kingdom is separate. He has His own plans, and those plans are "higher" than ours (Isa. 55:9). In fact, as we see in Jesus' prayer, God even hides His ways and His thoughts from those who are too smart for their own good.

If you want the answer to life's troubles, you need to surrender like an infant again. God reveals His plans, thoughts, and ways to those who, like infants, trust Him. An infant gives complete trust to whomever is caring for him or her. Similarly, we are to do the same spiritually if we want to know how to off-load our bitter burdens brought on by pain. Yet if you choose to depend upon your own degrees, your own pedigree, your own circle of friends to tell you what's what, you can carry your own garbage with you.

> Jesus offers a way to gain hope when you are hurting, but it only comes through Him.

Jesus offers a way to gain hope when you are hurting, but it only comes through Him. The answer is not located in your own knowledge, experience, success, or human wisdom. That is a man-made approach to solving life's situations. The secret that God hides from others but will make available to you when you seek Him comes in three words Jesus goes on to say: Come. Take. Learn.

Come

He starts off in Matthew 11:28 by calling the worn out and burdened to Him by saying, "Come to Me, all who are weary and heavy-laden, and I will give you rest." Come to Jesus. If you are weary, weighed down, and heavy-laden, Jesus asks that you first come to Him.

When the afflictions of life, the pains of the past, and the regrets of your yesteryears have piled high like the toxic trash on the *Pelicano*, you start to get rid of it by coming to Christ. Just come. Don't worry about cleaning yourself up first. Don't worry about getting your Sunday best on first. Don't worry about hiding your baggage under your bed. Just come to Christ.

Now, I want to point out that being weary is different from being sleepy. Sleepiness comes from the normal wear and tear of living as a human in this world. The body simply gets tired. What weariness does is interrupt your natural need for sleep. In fact, being weary will often keep you awake when you feel exhausted. Or, if you do manage to fall asleep, you find yourself the subject of your very own nightmare on Elm Street.

Jesus reminds us through this first step that when life has done a number on you, you have an open invitation to come to Him. When you do, you can expect what He says: He will give you rest. He will begin to remove the weight that holds you down. He will begin to relieve you of the nightmares that keep you from getting a good night's rest. He will help you rest well while you wait for your healing to come about.

> When life has done a number on you, you have an open invitation to come to Jesus.

This word *rest* is an important word in the Bible. It shows up all the way at the beginning of Scripture. We read that after God created the earth and divided the seas and produced the plant life and caused all things to grow and flourish, on the seventh day, He chose to rest.

Now, it doesn't tell us God chose to sleep. Rather, God rested. In our contemporary translation, we might say He sat back and enjoyed Himself. He chilled. He kicked up His anthropomorphic feet and took a deep anthropomorphic breath.[1]

So critical is this concept of rest that God told Israel to honor the Sabbath day every week through an intentional pursuit of rest. He had them pursue their work for six days every week, but on the seventh day they were instructed to rest. Knowing humanity's propensity to pursue more and more through hard work or finagling, He prohibited them to do so on the Sabbath. It wasn't just a suggestion; it was a command. God knew that they were not the source of their own gain anyhow. The Sabbath served as a reminder to them of what He already knew.

Scripture condemns workaholism or a tendency to neglect rest in preference to work when it says in Psalm 127:2: "It is vain for you to rise up early, to retire late, to eat the bread of painful labors; for He gives to His beloved even in his sleep." To rest is to trust. Resting means you are putting your worries and pain in God's hands and leaving them there. Hebrews 4:9 puts it like this: "So there remains a Sabbath rest for the people of God."

Another way to phrase it is to say that you can relax in Jesus' arms. He's got it. Whatever it is that consumes you right now or seeks to eat away at your emotions, just go to Jesus and let Him take care of it for you—in His way, not your own.

Thursday's my day. I don't know what your day is, but Thursday is trash day at the Evans's home. They used to come twice a week, but they reduced it to just Thursdays. Every Thursday morning, I have the trash out by the curb in plenty of time for them to pick it up. I don't want to miss them because then I'll be stuck with smelly, stinky trash for a whole other week. But you know one thing I have noticed about trash day? I have never had a trashman come up to my front door and ring the doorbell, asking me where my trash is. I have never had that happen. If it's not out there by the curb, they just move on. It's up to me to get it out there.

Likewise, it's up to you to carry your burden to Jesus. He says, "Come." He doesn't say to wait inside the confines of your own pain for Him to show up and take it all away. You need to take the step of bringing your emotional and spiritual trash to Him. When you carry your burden to Christ, He will give you rest. He will take it away. He will remove the stench causing you to remain awake when you should be asleep. He will cart off the load piling high in your soul, taking up too much room and limiting your spiritual life within. He will do all of this, but you have to do something first: *you have to carry your trash to Jesus Christ.*

Be careful not to do what so many of us do, which is simply called "trash management." That's when your trash piles up and you seek to get more trash to fit by pushing it down and making more room. Or maybe you have one of those old trash mashers that will crush your trash so you can fit more in. That may give you space for a season, but the stench will only continue to sour the atmosphere of your soul, and the weight bearing down on your heart will only increase.

To be free from the effects of emotional, mental, spiritual, and physical garbage, you've got to let it go. You've heard it before, I'm sure—"Let go and let God." It's easy to post on social media. Easier to say to a friend. But letting go of the pains life has allowed you to experience isn't always easy. Far too many people hold on to these pains and hurts as a badge of their own identity. They make their identity about what they have suffered rather than releasing it and facing each new day with a fresh perspective, content in who they are as a free child of the King. I've seen this happen in areas where victimization becomes its own idol. It is often easier to remain in the role of victim because it frees the person from personal responsibility. If there is always someone or something else to blame, then the real spiritual work of healing, growth, and maturity can be ignored.

Spiritual growth is not easy. Maturing as an individual is not easy. Neither is healing. But, once you set your mind to do it and you begin to taste the freedom and dignity it produces within, you will discover it is worth the effort required. Prolonged identification with oppression, victimization, or pain will only keep you in a loop of living as less than you were created to be. To do so ultimately gives whatever, or whomever, caused the hurt in the first place more power over you than ever before. To get back your own personal power, you need to let past pains go. Learn from them, but don't live in them.

In football, when the quarterback receives the ball from the center, he's immediately under pressure.

The defensive linemen come at him with a vengeance. They have one goal in mind: they want that ball. Whatever it takes to knock the quarterback down and get a sack is what they will try to do, within the rules of the game. The faster the quarterback can release the ball, the faster he will be free from the pursuit and the pressure.

See, the pressure isn't personal. It isn't about him. It's all about the ball. As soon as the quarterback throws the ball to a wideout or tight end, or hands it off to the running back or halfback, the pressure changes its direction. What once was an onslaught of defenders seeking to tear him down, tackle him, and destroy him, now sets their target elsewhere. They turn their gaze. They follow the ball.

Friend, as long as you are holding on to the ball of this life's pain, hurts, and struggles, you are going to feel the pressure. This is the "opportunity" Satan seeks to seize you in. But Jesus says if you will just hand the ball off to Him, He will take the heat for you. He will give you rest. You can wind up standing there on the field, as quarterbacks often do, while a play continues, observing the hits, tackles, and pain rather than absorbing them.

I'll never forget counseling a couple who was madly in love. They couldn't wait to get married. The problem was that the wife-to-be had accumulated a significant amount of debt and student loans. They just couldn't see how they could get married with all of that debt. That's when they came to me for counseling.

After hearing their dilemma, I turned to the man and asked him if he would be willing to take her debt. I asked him if he would be willing to pay it off for her over time. He thought about it and said, "Yes, absolutely." By doing so, he let her know that her burden was no longer hers to carry. As her husband, he was going to lighten that load.

Tears ran down her face as she felt the weight fall off. Jesus says that when you come to Him, you may be bringing a load, but He has plenty of love. If you will simply turn your load over to Him, He will carry it for you. He will figure out how to deal with it for you. He will lead you through the waters so that you will not succumb to the storm and drown (Isa. 43:2a). The rest Jesus offers you is a gift. It is His gift to you, if you will accept it, to relax as life goes on all around you.

Take

The second action Jesus asks us to do after we come is to "take." Matthew 11:29 puts it like this: "Take My yoke upon you and learn from Me, for I am gentle and humble in heart." To take something means you have to reach out to grab it. Just like you had to go to Jesus with your burden, He is now asking you to take what He offers to you—His yoke.

The time period in which Jesus made this statement was full of farmers. Thus, while many of us might think of an egg yolk when we hear the word *yoke*, Jesus' listeners knew exactly what He was referencing. He was talking of a harness that connects two farming animals together. Typically, a younger ox was paired with an older and stronger ox so that the younger ox could learn from the older.

The purpose of the yoke was threefold. First, it created companionship while the animals worked. Second, it taught the younger ox submission. Third, it allowed the weight of what was being pulled to fall upon the ox which could handle it best. Even though there were two oxen, they both did not pull the same weight. The stronger ox carried more of the burden.

When Jesus asks you to yoke up with Him, He is reminding you of His strength. He is reminding you that your burden and the weight that looms over you do not need to be pulled by you. If you will hook up with Him, He will do the work while you simply walk alongside Him in a spirit of surrender. You can enjoy the companionship He provides as Your Lord and Savior while He handles the hard stuff in your life.

If you have ever been stuck before, whether in mud or a ditch, you know the power of a harness. A harness can lift something that seemed immovable because it is attached to something else that has the power to do just that. Jesus puts it simply for us: when we come to Him and connect with Him by taking His yoke upon us, He gives rest, companionship, and an ease in all the things we need to do or go through in this life. But as long as you choose to go your own way, you will stay stuck. You will stay trapped. You will remain beneath the weight of your own burdens.

In order to take Jesus' yoke upon you, you need to hitch yourself to Him. Knowing who He is won't cut it. Talking about Him won't cut it either. Jesus gave a clear picture with the oxen's yoke of what we need to do to experience His power in our lives. It's not enough to be saved if you are hoping to experience the abundant life on earth. Yes, being saved will get you to heaven. But staying hitched gets heaven to you. Another way Jesus words this in a different passage is to "abide" (John 15:4). To abide means to hang out with and remain close to Christ by pursuing an intimate relationship with Him.

You and I both know how important abiding is when it comes to your phone. If your phone does not abide with its charger long enough, it will not have enough power and will die. This isn't a philosophical concept floating around in never-never land. When Jesus says we need to yoke up with Him, or abide in Him, He is letting us know where we go to remain charged. He is letting us know where we can get power. When troubling emotions give you a low-battery alert on life, you need to get connected to Christ in a closer way. Doing the "spiritual stuff" or "religious rituals" won't give you the power you need to heal from the hurts we all experience while on earth. The reason why they won't give you all you need is because they were never designed to! Jesus is the Source of your strength. Ephesians 6:10 puts it like this: "Finally, be strong in the Lord and in the strength of His might."

Second Timothy 2:1 also reminds us: "You therefore, my son, be strong in the grace that is in Christ Jesus." It is Jesus' might which is to be the source of our own. It is His strength and His grace which is to strengthen our own souls. We learn how to give ourselves grace for the sins and mistakes of the past when we experience the grace that is in Christ Jesus. We also learn the power of forgiving others through drawing near to the One who has forgiven all.

The young ox that was yoked to the other learned how to do what he needed to do through the process. The whole point of the yoke was development and maturation. Jesus desires that we remain yoked to Him so that we can learn how to live this life, make wise decisions, go in the right direction. He wants to draw us close to Him so He can tell us the secrets of God, the hidden things from ages ago, which will enable us to overcome the

> We learn how to give ourselves grace for the sins and mistakes of the past when we experience the grace that is in Christ Jesus.

schemes and strategies of Satan and to handle the suffering in our lives.

One of Satan's primary methods for getting a follower of Christ off the path he or she needs to be on is through emotional strongholds brought about through pain, hurt, or sadness. Jesus knows you need to be set free. That is why He has asked you to simply come to Him. Draw near to Him. Take His yoke upon you.

Learn

When you take His yoke upon you, you will be positioned to do the third and final thing He asks you to do in this passage: "learn" (Matt. 11:29). Learn from Him. Follow Him. Discover how Jesus responds to persecution, rebuke, slander, and the like. Witness how Jesus responds when life gives Him a burden to bear. What does His Spirit speak to your soul when you have an opportunity to respond to a difficulty yourself? Apply what you learn from Jesus, and you will find hope for any amount of hurt you face.

Jesus wants you to learn from Him about being gentle and humble in heart. He wants you to not simply admire that He is gentle and humble in heart;

He wants you to learn how to be gentle and humble in heart too. That's the key. That's what you need to know.

It is in gentleness and humility that you will find rest for your soul. If you allow this world and all of the injustices within it and all of the pains and things that are simply not fair within it to harden your heart, or agitate your heart, or disillusion your heart, you will be bound to your emotions. But if you learn from Jesus how to respond to life's challenges through gentleness, grace, and humility that reflect God's heart of love, you will unlock the door to fully living out your destiny. You will be free from the trap of emotional bondage so that you can pursue being who you were designed to be, to the glory of God and the good of others.

When Jesus speaks of His yoke being easy and His burden being light (v. 30), He is giving you the very wisdom you need to honor your life's pain while also releasing it through healing. One of the Greek interpretations of the word *easy* means custom-fit, or specially made. It's like having a custom-fit shirt as compared to one that you buy off the rack at any store. A custom-fit shirt is made for your size and dimensions. It will look right on you. A custom-made approach to heal-ing your heart is what Jesus offers if you will draw near enough to learn from Him how to do it.

There is no one-size-fits-all solution to broken hearts burdened with life's pain. I wish there were. I would preach it every Sunday. But the path to your peace is *your* path. It's a custom path. I can't tell you which way to go in order to find healing and calm, other than to go to the One who knows which way you should go. You'll need to listen to Him because He has a unique plan for lifting you up out of the toxic ashes of life's pain.

Now, before I close this chapter, I want to remind you that Jesus isn't promising to take all your burdens away. What He is saying is they won't weigh the same for you anymore. You won't have to carry them alone anymore. Jesus said your burden, if you come to Him, take His yoke upon you, and learn from Him, will be light.

I was going through the airport on my way to a flight one day when I had one suitcase in each hand. They were starting to get heavy as I carried them. But then someone pointed out to me that they had wheels on the bottom of them. I had forgotten and had lifted them both up to carry. As soon as I put them down and pulled out the handles to roll them, my burden got light! The weight didn't change; rather, how I interacted with the weight and the burden of the bags changed. What once had caused me to sweat and grunt and struggle now glided easily along the floor.

Jesus' promise in this passage isn't that you will have no problems. He doesn't promise your pain or issues will magically disappear. He doesn't promise a world of peace or prosperity. But He does promise that how you feel about it will be very different. How you interact with the burden and the weight will be very different. How far you can go while still bearing it will be very different. You won't get tired out from the load you carry in this life. Jesus promises you His rest.

Our world has many problems that show up in our lives in every shape and size. There is a list of things to worry about before you even open your eyes for the morning. Rest is becoming more and more of a luxury for people—the kind of rest which means calm, peace, internal stability. But that is exactly what Jesus will give you if you seek Him.

So important is this gift of rest that Jesus emphasized it again as He closed out what He was saying.

He concludes His call to come, take His yoke, and learn by saying, "YOU WILL FIND REST FOR YOUR SOULS. For My yoke is easy and My burden is light" (Matt. 11:29a–30).

At first, when He started out, Jesus said He would give you rest. But here toward the end, He changes it a bit by saying, "You will find rest." That's a different statement. God can do both. He can give and you can find it. If you come to Him, He will give it to you at some level. But when you take His yoke and learn from Him and follow His ways based on what you learned, He will help you locate the additional rest. You'll get a greater grace. You'll receive a personal peace. You'll experience an increased intimacy with the Source of rest Himself. And couldn't we all use a bit more rest right now?

Two men had entered a forester competition to see who could cut down the most trees in a day. One of the men was much older, and by looking at the two men, you would assume the younger man would win without much of a battle. He had youth on his side. He had strength on his side. It didn't appear to even be a question how this competition would wind up.

Every hour or so as they were chopping trees, the older man would go get a drink of water and sit down. He would sit there for about ten minutes and rest. The younger man kept chopping down trees, chuckling to himself as he thought of the prize money he would soon claim. He took no breaks, and the older man fell farther behind in the competition. He just kept chopping steady, one tree after the other. But the older man consistently took his ten-minute break every hour to rest.

At the end of the day, when it came time to count the number of trees that had been chopped down, the judges stated that the older man had chopped down twice as many trees as the younger guy. The younger man said, "I don't understand! You kept stopping to rest. How on earth did you chop down twice as much as me?"

To which the older man replied, "Well, it's fairly simple. What you didn't notice was that every time I took my break, I was sharpening my ax."

When you've got the right tool working for you, you can afford to take a rest. When your ax blade is sharper than the next guy's, you can sit down for a while. When you take Jesus' yoke upon you so that He can carry the burden of the hurt and pain you have been carrying for so long, you can relax. You can go further. You can last longer. You can contribute more. You can breathe more freely.

I know your pain feels paralyzing to you at times. I know the situation you face in your marriage or your singlehood, with your health, in your job, or with your finances can seem as if it will take every ounce of strength you have to give just to survive. But if you will come close to Jesus and hook up with Him, He will whisper something important in your ear. Can you hear Him?

"I've got it," He says. "I've got it. You can rest, just knowing I've got this for you."

Rest.

CHAPTER 6

Turning Bitter to Sweet

You know it's a bad day when you wake up in the morning hearing birds outside your window, only to open the curtains and see it is a group of buzzards.

Many of us seem to be stuck in an unending loop of bad days. We hope that an entry into a new year will somehow remove the difficulties of the previous year, but we find out it's just a flip on the calendar—nothing more and nothing less. So we look ahead to the next holiday to somehow make things better, or the next vacation, or the next visit to church. Anything, really. We just want to break the cycle of bad days.

Hopelessness comes when a string of bad days piles up so high they seem to reach the sky. I know what that is like, personally. You probably know what it is like as well. Just a quick glance at our culture and our world, and we see that a lot of people know what it's like. It's as if we are all experiencing our own personal earthquakes, which lead to our own personal tsunamis, which then flood everyone else simultaneously.

I've seen my fair share of the already short fuses of anger and prejudices in some people I know over these past few years become even shorter. I've seen patience wear thin. Optimism get snuffed out. Sighs become the norm, while smiles get lost in the grief—grief over a lost normalcy for so many. A lost hope. Just when it looks like something might be going to turn the corner in our lives, churches, or culture, a new punch is thrown. A new disappointment comes about. It's enough to cause people to lose belief in the possibility of a better day.

The Israelites knew this too. They were overjoyed with their freedom from slavery, only to find themselves pressed up against the Red Sea with an enemy in pursuit. Once through, they were so overjoyed again that they burst out in song, only to find themselves hungry and thirsty in the wilderness. In fact, when someone spotted water up ahead, they gave in to their hope and became so overjoyed that they had found water at all, that they celebrated on the way to it. Yet once they drank the water, they realized it was bitter, and they had to spit it out.

When life gets sour, bitter, and toxic, you feel as if you must spew it out. Your stomach is unsettled. You walk around with what feels like a knot in your gut, keeping you from feeling at ease. Sometimes this bitter water leads to real physical problems that manifest in your body. Emotional and spiritual disease is one of the leading contributors to physical disease. So, what do you do when your hope has gone on a roller-coaster, only to keep dropping further and further once you reach the top of every hill? We can take notes from what God did for the Israelites when they came upon the bitter waters of Marah. God addressed their situation in a unique way, and through a look at what He did for them, we can gain discernment and insight into what He can do for each of us.

The story is found in Exodus 15. We set the stage with verses 20–24. You'll see the quick change in emotions from singing praises to God to grumbling at God in just a matter of moments. It says:

> Miriam the prophetess, Aaron's sister, took the timbrel in her hand, and all the women went out after her with timbrels and with dancing. Miriam answered them,
>
> "Sing to the LORD, for He is highly exalted; the horse and his rider He has hurled into the sea."
>
> Then Moses led Israel from the Red Sea, and they went out into the wilderness of Shur; and they went three days in the wilderness and found no water. When they came to Marah, they could not drink the waters of Marah, for they were bitter; therefore it was named Marah. So the people grumbled at Moses, saying, "What shall we drink?"

The Israelites went from praising to complaining about as fast as possible. At first, they thanked God for opening the waters and allowing them to pass through. Then they grumbled at God for leading them to water that was bitter. It's almost as if they started complaining once they hit the parking lot after church.

Has that ever happened to you? You feel the fullness of the Spirit and the joy of the Lord during a worship service, only to reach your car and get upset with the driver in front of you who stops too quickly or cuts in. Our emotions can go from high to low a lot faster than we would like to admit, which is exactly what happened to the Israelites.

Throughout the Old Testament, you will find God—in a multiplicity of ways—reminding His people that He was the One who delivered them out of Egypt. The reason why He reminded them is so that when they ran into a new problem, a new hurt or disappointment, they would not lose sight of the old. They would not forget that God delivered them back then.

The great danger when life gets bitter—when you run into the waters of Marah—is to forget what God did yesterday. Now, we can't live in yesterday. I'm not saying that you should always be focusing on the past. But neither are we to forget the faithfulness of God and the things He did yesterday. We need to set up our own stones of remembrance so that we do not forget His past actions and deliverance on our behalf (see Josh. 4:20–24). I want to stress this because I know that what you may be going through right now has the propensity to suck you dry of any hope for tomorrow. In fact, it can suck you so dry that you forget that while circumstances may change, God does not.

The Israelites had forgotten that all-important truth. They were new on their journey of faith. Once they found the bitter water which they could not drink to satisfy their thirst, they complained. They argued. They grumbled. In essence, they went to their leader, Moses, and demanded he fix it or take them back to Egypt. This was not the freedom they were hoping for. So Moses went from praise to problem to prayer. Exodus 15:25 tells us: "Then he cried out to the Lord."

> While circumstances may change, God does not.

Whenever the Bible talks about "crying out," it's not referring to a simple prayer. It's not talking about saying grace before a meal. To cry out to God implies that you are desperate. Your situation is serious. You need Him to intervene. Moses has almost two million people under his charge who are thirsty. Their bodies need water. But the water they found is undrinkable.

Moses has the potential of having the people he just led to freedom die from dehydration. Of course, he cried out. And after he did, God showed him His plan.

God instructed Moses to throw a tree into the waters to purify it. We read the rest of verse 25: "and the LORD showed him a tree; and he threw it into the waters, and the waters became sweet." When Moses cried out to God, God showed him the solution to his problem at hand. Keep in mind, God did not show him the solution until he cried out. Also keep in mind, the solution seemed a little . . . weird. But isn't that how God can work at times?

I know most pastors won't openly call God's ways weird, but if we were honest, they do come across that way at times. Who would have thought that holding up a stick would cause a sea to divide? And who would have thought that tossing a tree into bitter water would make it sweet? Those are new strategies to most of us. Some might even consider them strange. That is why it's critical that as you and I work through the healing of life's hurts, we stick close to God. His plan to make the bitter waters sweet won't be the same for everyone, and it probably won't be a plan you would have thought up on your own.

It is in staying near to God and crying out to Him rather than complaining to others that you will learn the pathway to relief and peace.

Sweet Water

After turning the water sweet, God reminded the Israelites once again what their trust in Him would gain them. We read as the story continues: "There He made for them a statute and regulation, and there He tested them. And He said, 'If you will give earnest heed to the voice of the LORD your God, and do what is right in His sight, and give ear to His command-ments, and keep all His statutes, I will put none of the diseases on you which I have put on the Egyptians; for I, the LORD, am your healer'" (Exod. 15:25b–26).

God sought to solidify their faith through estab-lishing a statute and regulation. He laid out for them the cause-and-effect scenario they could come to expect from Him. He wasn't hiding His plan or their pathway to promise. After turning the water sweet so that they could live, once again freed from certain disaster, He reminded them that He would care for them if they would just "give earnest heed to the voice of the LORD your God, and do what is right in His sight, and give ear to His commandments, and keep all His statutes" (v. 26). In essence, He was foreshadowing a choice He would soon give them: *choose life, that you and your families may live* (Deut. 30:19–20).

Free will affords each of us an opportunity known as choice. We get to choose the actions we make, thoughts we think, and words we say—all of which come with consequences built in. If you choose to wallow in self-pity and self-defeating thoughts and words, don't be surprised if your life reflects that. If you choose to doubt God and seek to come up with your own solutions to numb your hurt, then don't be surprised when once the numbness wears off, the pain is even worse than before.

God has set before each of us the free will to choose. We can complain. He's given us that option. We can give up. He's also given us that option. We can throw in the towel. God is not going to force anyone to believe in Him or to act like it either. But when you make those choices and fail to throw the tree into the bitter water because you would rather complain at how bitter the water has become, then don't blame

God when the water remains bitter. That was your choice.

God gets far more blame for things that are our fault than He ever could deserve. God doesn't owe you sweet water while you grumble and doubt Him. He promises sweet water if you will "give earnest heed to the voice of the LORD your God, and do what is right in His sight, and give ear to His commandments, and keep all His statutes" (Exod. 15:26). When you choose to toss the tree into the bitter waters of your day—to do whatever it is God is asking you to do, no matter how weird it may seem to you—that's when you will see the water turn sweet. That's when you will experience God's healing for your hurt. But the experience of His healing power only shows up in the situations that call for it. To experience His deliverance requires that you know you *need* to be delivered.

The only time you truly know the value and strength of an anchor is in a storm. It is when the waters around you are causing you to shake to the point that you can no longer stand on your own. That's when you see God show up. In fact, nothing will make God more real to you than Marah. Nothing will make God more real to you than those times when what you thought was a blessing turns bitter. Maybe it's a job that has turned bitter, or a marriage, or a friendship—your health, finances, our nation, our culture—any number of things.

When things get bitter, your view of God can get bigger than ever before—if and when you cry out to Him and then do what He says to do. God is often doing His greatest work when He is nowhere to be found. He does some of His best work in the dark. In those times when you don't think He is doing a thing, God's up to something great behind the scenes. But He's waiting for you to call out to Him so He can reveal the pathway to sweeter waters.

In those times when you don't think He is doing a thing, God's up to something great behind the scenes.

God longs to bring you and me into deeper experiences with Him. He does this because He knows that it is in those seasons of struggle that we learn how strong He truly is. He wants to take the Bible off of the pages of paper and put it into the everyday-ness of your reality. You may know the Word of God, but He wants you to experience the words of God speaking to your spirit right now. He speaks to you through His Spirit.

I understand you may be disappointed. I know you are hurting—especially if you picked up this book. I know you thought God had provided a way, only to discover that the water was bitter and didn't really taste good after all. You may even be scared to say it out loud. So I'll say it for you. Perhaps you are thinking thoughts like:

God, you have disappointed me.

God, You have let me down.

You have failed me.

I can't find You right now.

Yet, when God is nowhere to be found is precisely when He is the closest nearby. He may be silent, but He is not still. As bad as you may feel, I urge you to turn to Him. Instead of complaining, cry out to Him. Instead of fixating on today's pain, remember yesterday's provisions. God didn't show the tree to the complainers. He showed it to Moses, the man who cried out.

You get to choose right now what you will do as you face life's pain and your heart's hurt. Are you going to continue down the pathway of complaining, sulking, blaming, and dreading each new day? Or are you going to turn to God? I know life may be sorrowful. Trust me, I know it firsthand. It can even feel crazy at times. But in the midst of it all, God reminds us that He is testing us. In fact, He says it as clearly as it can be said in Deuteronomy 8:2: "You shall remember all the way which the LORD your God has led you in the wilderness these forty years, that He might humble you, testing you, to know what was in your heart, whether you would keep His commandments or not."

> Are you going to continue down the pathway of complaining, sulking, blaming, and dreading each new day? Or are you going to turn to God?

He wants to see whether you will trust Him in the dark, when the bitter waters aim to overwhelm you like a flood. When your life itself turns sour and your tears sting, will you cry out to God and do what He asks you to do? Or will you sit, soak, and sour in your pain, allowing the bitterness of the water to turn your own heart bitter as well?

Let me tell you what often happens to us when we reach places like Marah—seasons of bitterness. We attribute to men what was really caused, or allowed, by God. In other words, we blame people. The Israelites grumbled at Moses and pointed their fingers at him, yet just a few verses earlier, they were praising God for His deliverance. Like a football coach, Moses didn't get any credit for a win but took all the blame for a loss. One of the reasons we do this is because it's easier to get to people and blame them. It's harder to get to God. Plus, most people are too scared of God to blame Him for anything!

As we near the close of our time together in this book, I want to challenge you to ask God to show you your tree. Ask Him to reveal to you what it is He wants you to toss into the bitter waters of your soul in order to make the water sweet. Go to God for your next steps. He is your Source. He is your Provider. He is your Healer. Learn from these moments in life where God allows you to suffer. Learn how to depend on Him even more. Learn how to look for His hand of deliverance and His way of release. It is in these situations of life that you get to know God for yourself.

The Old Testament believer Job learned this. His lot was hard—probably much harder than yours or mine. Yet he held onto God and worshiped Him through the suffering. And after it was over, Job knew God better. He got to know God for himself. In Job's own words: "I have heard of You by the hearing of the ear; but now my eye sees You" (Job 42:5).

God will often allow us to go through difficult scenarios in order to test what is in our hearts. He wants to know if you truly believe what you say you believe. He isn't doing it to be mean. But He also isn't doing it as if He's not really sure. God knows everything. He is doing it to reveal *to you* those areas where you still may need to grow and strengthen your faith. He also wants *you* to know what is in your heart.

Oftentimes you cannot know until you are put to the test. You cannot know a person's character until that person is put through the fire. In other words, God wants to show you your heart too. He wants you to know the truth of who you are in order to develop you.

A test is a negative situation that God allows to take place in your life for the purpose of moving you to the next spiritual level. Thus, when you come to the waters of Marah and you discover that they are bitter, rather than fuss about what you are facing, turn to God to reveal to you the tree He will use to reverse the difficulty in your life. God will walk you through the bitter situations of this life in order to strengthen your faith in Him. But never forget that God always provides pit stops in the wilderness. Whether it's in parting the Red Sea or turning the bitter water sweet or even in providing an oasis of water and food (Exod. 15:27) or water from a rock (Exod. 17:6) or manna from above (Exod. 16:1–21), He provides along the way.

> God will walk you through the bitter situations of this life in order to strengthen your faith in Him.

The wilderness of our lives is not the promised land. The promised land flows with milk and honey. You will abound in plenty in the promised land. But in the wilderness times, when life becomes dry and your heart becomes bitter, God creates pit stops. He offers a watering hole. He offers you a place of refuge where you can pause and regain your strength so that you can start out on your way to the next pit stop.

Keep in mind, a pit stop is not the promised land either. It's not the ultimate goal. It is a place to refuel so that you can get closer to where you are headed. When you drive across country, you can't just drive from one side of the nation to the other. You can't skip the gas stations altogether and plan to make it. You have to stop and refuel. Similarly, when you are in a hurting situation in your life, God gives you spots and seasons to refuel. Sometimes it's God Himself showing you what you can do. Other times it may be a kind and encouraging word from someone. Sometimes it's a respite you discover in a relationship which pours wisdom into your thinking. It could be a song, a book, a walk in nature. Whatever it is, God will give you what you need to keep going.

We are all on a journey. We're at different places in our journey, but we are all in this thing called life together. The temptation to complain, blame, and grumble when things don't go our way is there for each of us. But it is in those times that it is most important to hold on to God like never before. Wrap your heart around His hope with a faith that you have never shown before.

There are times in your life when faith will be all you have. These dark nights in our lives make it seem like even God has backed away from us. He's put the transmission in reverse, and your life is spiraling. But God reminds us through the stories we have looked at in these pages that it is in those times that He wants us to embrace His statutes, ordinances, and commands the most. He wants you to reach out and embrace Him and His Word, His will, and His agenda. He wants you to discover for yourself that He is your healer and provider.

When life just doesn't seem to be working for you, draw near to God.

When all hope seems gone, cry out to Him.

Don't just depend on doctrine and memorized passages to get you through. Lean on God Himself. It's one thing to say He is a Waymaker. But it's another thing entirely to experience Him making a way.

He is able to transform your hurt into hope again. Ask Him to do that right now.

The Urban Alternative

The Urban Alternative (TUA) equips, empowers, and unites Christians to impact *individuals, families, churches,* and *communities* through a thoroughly kingdom-agenda worldview. In teaching truth, we seek to transform lives.

The core cause of the problems we face in our personal lives, homes, churches, and societies is a spiritual one; therefore, the only way to address it is spiritually. We've tried a political, social, economic, and even a religious agenda.

It's time for a **kingdom agenda**.

> *The kingdom agenda can be defined as the visible manifestation of the comprehensive rule of God over every area of life.*

The unifying central theme throughout the Bible is the glory of God and the advancement of His kingdom. The conjoining thread from Genesis to Revelation—from beginning to end—is focused on one thing: God's glory through advancing God's kingdom.

When you do not recognize that theme, the Bible becomes disconnected stories that are great for inspiration but seem to be unrelated in purpose and direction. Understanding the role of the kingdom in Scripture increases the relevancy of this several thousand-year-old text to your day-to-day living, because the kingdom is not only then, it is now.

The absence of the kingdom's influence in our personal lives, family lives, churches, and communities has led to a deterioration in our world of immense proportions:

- People live segmented, compartmentalized lives because they lack God's kingdom worldview.
- Families disintegrate because they exist for their own satisfaction rather than for the kingdom.
- Churches are limited in the scope of their impact because they fail to comprehend that the goal of the church is not the church itself, but the kingdom.
- Communities have nowhere to turn to find real solutions for real people who have real problems because the church has become divided, ingrown, and unable to transform the cultural and political landscape in any relevant way.

The kingdom agenda offers us a way to see and live life with a solid hope by optimizing the solutions of heaven. When God is no longer the final and authoritative standard under which all else falls, order and hope leaves with Him. But the reverse of that is true as well: as long as you have God, you have hope.

If God is still in the picture, and as long as His agenda is still on the table, it's not over.

Even if relationships collapse, God will sustain you. Even if finances dwindle, God will keep you. Even if dreams die, God will revive you. As long as God, and His rule, are still the overarching standard in your life, family, church, and community, there is always hope.

Our world needs the King's agenda. Our churches need the King's agenda. Our families need the King's agenda.

We've put together a three-part plan to direct us to heal the divisions and strive for unity as we move toward the goal of truly being one nation under God. This three-part plan calls us to assemble with others in unity, address the issues that divide us, and to act together for social impact. Following this plan, we will see individuals, families, churches, and communities transformed as we follow God's kingdom agenda in every area of our lives. You can request this plan by sending an email to info@tonyevans.org or by going online to tonyevans.org.

In many major cities, there is a loop that drivers can take when they want to get somewhere on the other side of the city, but don't necessarily want to head straight through downtown. This loop will take you close enough to the city so that you can see its towering buildings and skyline, but not close enough to actually experience it.

This is precisely what we, as a culture, have done with God. We have put Him on the "loop" of our personal, family, church, and community lives. He's close enough to be at hand should we need Him in an emergency, but far enough away that He can't be the center of who we are.

We want God on the "loop," not the King of the Bible who comes downtown into the very heart of our ways. Leaving God on the "loop" brings about dire consequences as we have seen in our own lives and with others. But when we make God, and His rule, the centerpiece of all we think, do, or say, it is then that we will experience Him in the way He longs for us to experience Him.

He wants us to be kingdom people with kingdom minds set on fulfilling His kingdom's purposes. He wants us to pray, as Jesus did, "not My will, but Yours be done" (Luke 22:42). Because His is the kingdom, the power, and the glory (Matt. 6:13).

There is only one God, and we are not Him. As King and Creator, God calls the shots. It is only when we align ourselves underneath His comprehensive hand that we will access His full power and authority in all spheres of life: personal, familial, ecclesiastical, and governmental.

As we learn how to govern ourselves under God, we then transform the institutions of family, church, and society using a biblically based kingdom worldview.

*Under Him, we touch heaven
and change earth.*

To achieve our goal, we use a variety of strategies, approaches, and resources for reaching and equipping as many people as possible.

Broadcast Media

Millions of individuals experience *The Alternative with Dr. Tony Evans* through the daily radio broadcast playing on nearly **1,400 radio outlets** and in more than **130 countries**. The broadcast can also be seen on several television networks and is available online at tonyevans.org. You can also listen to or view the daily broadcast by downloading the Tony Evans app for free in the App store. More than 30 million message downloads/streams occur each year.

Leadership Training

The Tony Evans Training Center (TETC) facilitates a comprehensive discipleship platform, which provides an educational program that embodies the ministry philosophy of Dr. Tony Evans as expressed through the kingdom agenda. The training courses focus on leadership development and discipleship in the following five tracks:

- Bible and Theology
- Personal Growth
- Family and Relationships
- Church Health and Leadership Development
- Society and Community Impact Strategies

The TETC program includes courses for both local and online students. Furthermore, TETC programming includes coursework for nonstudent attendees. Pastors, Christian leaders, and Christian laity, both local and at a distance, can seek out The

Kingdom Agenda Certificate for personal, spiritual, and professional development. For more information, visit: TonyEvansTraining.org.

The Kingdom Agenda Pastors (KAP) provides a *viable network* for *like-minded pastors* who embrace the kingdom-agenda philosophy. Pastors have the opportunity to go deeper with Dr. Tony Evans as they are given greater biblical knowledge, practical applications, and resources to impact individuals, families, churches, and communities. KAP welcomes *senior and associate pastors* of all churches. KAP also offers an annual Summit held each year in Dallas, with intensive seminars, workshops, and resources. For more information, visit: KAFellowship.org.

Pastors' Wives Ministry, founded by Dr. Lois Evans, provides *counsel, encouragement,* and *spiritual resources* for pastors' wives as they serve with their husbands in the ministry. A primary focus of the ministry is the KAP Summit that offers senior pastors' wives a safe place to *reflect, renew,* and *relax* along with training in personal development, spiritual growth, and care for their emotional and physical well-being. For more information, visit: LoisEvans.org.

Kingdom Community Impact

The outreach programs of The Urban Alternative seek to provide positive impact to individuals, churches, families, and communities through a variety of ministries. We see these efforts as necessary to our calling as a ministry and essential to the communities we serve. With training on how to initiate and maintain programs to adopt schools, or provide homeless services, or partner toward unity and justice with the local police precincts, which creates a connection between the police and our community, we, as a ministry, live out God's kingdom agenda according to our *Kingdom Strategy for Community Transformation*.

The *Kingdom Strategy for Community Transformation* is a three-part plan that equips churches to have a positive impact on their communities for the kingdom of God. It also provides numerous practical suggestions for how this three-part plan can be implemented in your community, and it serves as a blueprint for unifying churches around the common goal of creating a better world for all of us. For more information, visit: TonyEvans.org and click on the link to access the three-part plan.

National Church Adopt-a-School Initiative (NCAASI) prepares churches across the country to impact communities by using *public schools as the primary vehicle for effecting positive social change* in urban youth and families. Leaders of churches, school districts, faith-based organizations, and other nonprofit organizations are equipped with the knowledge and tools to *forge partnerships* and build *strong social service delivery systems.* This training is based on the comprehensive church-based community impact strategy conducted by Oak Cliff Bible Fellowship. It addresses such areas as economic development, education, housing, health revitalization, family renewal, and racial reconciliation. We assist churches in tailoring the model to meet specific needs of their communities while simultaneously addressing the spiritual and moral frame of reference. Training events are held annually in the Dallas area at Oak Cliff Bible Fellowship. For more information, visit: ChurchAdoptaSchool.org.

Athlete's Impact (AI) exists as an outreach both into and through the sports arena. Coaches can be the most influential factor in young people's lives, even ahead of their parents. With the growing rise of fatherlessness in our culture, more young people are looking to their coaches for guidance, character development, practical needs, and hope. After coaches on the influencer scale fall athletes. Athletes (whether professional or amateur) influence younger athletes and kids within their spheres of impact. Knowing this, we have made it our aim to equip and train coaches and athletes on how to live out and utilize their God-given roles for the benefit of the kingdom. We aim to do this through our iCoach App as well as resources such as *The Playbook: A Life Strategy Guide for Athletes*. For more information, visit: ICoachApp.org.

Tony Evans Films ushers in positive life change through compelling video shorts, animation, and feature-length films. We seek to build kingdom disciples through the power of story. We use a variety of platforms for viewer consumption and have more than 10 millon+ digital views. We also merge video-shorts and film with relevant Bible study materials to bring people to the saving knowledge of Jesus Christ and to strengthen the body of Christ worldwide. *Tony Evans Films* released its first feature-length film, *Kingdom Men Rising*, in April 2019 in over 800 theaters nationwide, in partnership with Lifeway Films.

The second release, *Journey with Jesus*, is in partnership with RightNow Media.

Resource Development

We are fostering lifelong learning partnerships with the people we serve by providing a variety of published materials. Dr. Evans has published more than 125 unique titles based on more than fifty years of preaching, whether that is in booklet, book, or Bible study format. He also holds the honor of writing and publishing the first full-Bible commentary and study Bible by an African American, released in 2019. This Bible sits in permanent display as a historic release, in The Museum of the Bible in Washington, D.C.

For more information, and a complimentary copy of Dr. Evans's devotional newsletter, call (800) 800–3222 *or* write TUA at P.O. Box 4000, Dallas TX 75208, *or* visit us online at www.TonyEvans.org.

NOTES

1. An *anthropomorphism* is a description of God in human terms. In other words, we know God doesn't really have "feet" or take "deep breaths," but it helps you get a good sense of what the Scripture is communicating.

Offer hope for the hurting

Do you want others to find comfort from God during difficult times? Share the message of this book with your small group. The *Hope for the Hurting* Bible study uses teaching videos and personal study to help participants (and other people they may meet) see pain and hurt through a biblical perspective.

The *Hope for the Hurting Leader Kit* includes:
- One *Bible Study Book*
- One DVD with six 10- to 12-minute video teaching sessions from Tony Evans
- Code for digital downloads
- The original book

Available wherever books are sold

Life is busy,
but Bible study is still possible.

a **portable** seminary

Explore the kingdom.
Anytime, anywhere.

TONY EVANS
TRAINING CENTER

tonyevanstraining.org

*Subscription model

Tony EVANS
THE URBAN ALTERNATIVE

YOUR *Eternity* IS OUR *Priority*

At The Urban Alternative, eternity is our priority—for the individual, the family, the church and the nation. The 45-year teaching ministry of Tony Evans has allowed us to reach a world in need with:

The Alternative – Our flagship radio program brings hope and comfort to an audience of millions on over 1,400 radio outlets across the country.

tonyevans.org – Our library of teaching resources provides solid Bible teaching through the inspirational books and sermons of Tony Evans.

Tony Evans Training Center – Experience the adventure of God's Word with our online classroom, providing at-your-own-pace courses for your PC or mobile device.

Tony Evans app – Packed with audio and video clips, devotionals, Scripture readings and dozens of other tools, the mobile app provides inspiration on-the-go.

**Explore God's kingdom today.
Live for more than the moment.
Live for *eternity*.**

tonyevans.org